DUNSHAY

Reflections on a DORSET MANOR HOUSE

DR ANDREW NORMAN

HALSGROVE

First published in Great Britain in 2004

Front cover picture: *'Dunshay Manor', from an original watercolour painting by John Grant.*

British Library Cataloguing-in-Publication Data
A CIP record for this title is available from the British Library

ISBN 1 84114 403 7

HALSGROVE

Halsgrove House
Lower Moor Way
Tiverton, Devon EX16 6SS
Tel: 01884 243242
Fax: 01884 243325
email: sales@halsgrove.com
website: www.halsgrove.com

Printed and bound by
The Cromwell Press, Trowbridge

Please note: Dunshay Manor is not normally open to the public. Viewing is strictly by appointment only.

Contents

Acknowledgements

I am grateful to the following for their encouragement and for sharing with me information, photographs and documents.

Mary Spencer Watson; the late Leslie Everett Baynes; Nigel W.E. Baynes; The Very Reverend Derek Watson, Dean of Salisbury; Suzanne Eward, M.A., F.S.A., A.L.A., Keeper of the Muniments, Salisbury Cathedral; Sara Rodger, Assistant Librarian, Arundel Castle Trustees Ltd.; Treleven Haysom of St Aldhelm's Quarry; Liz Agnew of Corfe Castle Model Village and Gardens; Warren Molloy sculptor and stone-cutter; George Willey; Shropshire Records and Research Centre; Dr E. John Welton, Chairman, Montgomery Civic Society; The *Lancet*, for permission to quote from 'Medical Annotations' (September 13, 1862); Jessica Sutcliffe; BAE Systems, Farnborough, Hants; Russell-Cotes Art Gallery and Museum, Bournemouth; Valerie Newton (a descendant of Anna Sewell); Antique Collectors' Club Ltd., Woodbridge, Suffolk; Barry Rolfe, Secretary, British Gliding Associaton; David Messum Gallery, London W1.

Also to Bill and Vera Jesty of Bere Regis; Bernard and Joan Jesty of Weymouth; G.W. and M. Pike of Downshay Farm; Peter Devlin; Tessa Gigg of Upbury Farm, Yetminster; the Reverend Dudley Ratcliffe, Rector of Swanage; the Reverend Robert Watton, Rector of Worth; Jessica Sutcliffe.

I also gratefully acknowledge the help of Jean Norman, Joan Jordan, Michael Dragffy; and I am especially grateful to Rachel Dragffy, for all her helpful comments and suggestions; and to Mary Spencer Watson for allowing me to tell the story.

About the Author

Andrew Norman was born in Newbury, Berkshire, England in 1943. In 1956 his family moved to Southern Rhodesia (now Zimbabwe) and so witnessed the closing years of the colonial era. In 1959 the family returned to England, and in 1962 he went up to Oxford University, to St Edmund Hall. Having graduated in physiology he became a medical student at The Radcliffe Infirmary. He qualified as a doctor in 1970. He married in 1967 and has a son and daughter. In 1972 he went into general practice in Poole, Dorset. A serious back injury in 1983 forced his early retirement: he is now a writer.

His other books include:

HMS Hood: *Pride of the Royal Navy* – Stackpole Books, Mechanicsburg, P.A. U.S.A. (2001) – ISBN 0-8117-0789-X.

By Swords Divided: Corfe Castle in the Civil War – Halsgrove, Tiverton, U.K. (2003) – ISBN 1-84114-228-X.

Robert Mugabe and the Betrayal of Zimbabwe – McFarland & Company, Inc. Publishers, Jefferson, North Carolina, U.S.A. (2004) – ISBN 0-7864-1686-6.

T.E. Lawrence: Unravelling the Enigma – Halsgrove, Tiverton, U.K. (2003) – ISBN 1-84114-321-9.

Tyneham: the Lost Village of Dorset – Halsgrove, Tiverton, U.K. (2003) – ISBN 1-84114-322-7.

Thomas Hardy: Behind the Inscrutable Smile – Halsgrove, Tiverton, U.K. (2004) – ISBN 1-84114-324-3.

Sir Francis Drake: Behind the Pirate's Mask – Halsgrove, Tiverton, U.K. (2004) – ISBN 1-84114-371-5.

Preface

Dunshay Manor: the east front. Photo: Mary Spencer Watson.

Old houses have a fascination all of their own, but if they are also, or have been in the past, associated with equally fascinating, or even famous people, then this makes their attraction irresistible. Such a house is Dunshay Manor, set at the end of a leafy lane, in a quiet area of South Dorset known as the 'Isle of Purbeck'. The 'Isle' – which is not actually an island at all! – consists of heathland, forests, the Purbeck Hills, scattered hamlets, and some fine coastal scenery.

Miss Mary Spencer Watson, the present incumbent, remembers the first time she saw Dunshay Manor. She and her late parents George and Hilda – who loved to go exploring – had ridden there on horseback from Studland, the little coastal village near Swanage.

They learned later that 'Dunshay' is the original name for the house and Manor (being the one used by the Reverend John Hutchins, Rector of Holy Trinity Church, Wareham in his *The History and Antiquities of the County of Dorset*, which was published in 1774; the year after his death). The name derives from the Old English word 'dun' meaning 'a down' and 'hayes' which has the same derivation as the Old English word 'Hege' meaning an enclosure. The farm on the other hand is called 'Downshay'.

Suddenly, there it was, an ancient building of Purbeck stone with twin gables and elegant front gates with finials. They fell in love with it immediately, this enchanting house which was to be their home, and their retreat. It was 1923 and Mary was ten years old.

The landscape around Dunshay positively oozes with history; Corfe, formerly a royal castle but now a ruin; Studland, which once swarmed with pirates; and Tyneham and Kimmeridge which were the haunt of smugglers. Nevertheless, when Mary set out to discover whether there was any interesting history attached to her own house Dunshay Manor, she was astonished at what she managed to unearth, for it is true to say that numbered amongst its previous inhabitants are those who have made outstanding contributions in the fields of architecture (Alice Briwere), medicine (Benjamin Jesty), art (George Spencer Watson; Lucy Kemp Welch), sculpture (Mary Spencer Watson) and aviation (Leslie Baynes) which have been of benefit not only locally, but to mankind in general.

There is an old saying: that 'walls have ears'. However, if the walls of Dunshay Manor could also speak, then it is to be hoped that you would hear a similar story to the one which is about to unfold! The action takes place over several centuries; from the twelfth up to the present time.

'Portrait of a Painter': Self portrait by George Spencer Watson R.A. – Exhibited Hampstead Art Galley 1920 and Fine Arts Society, 1934.
Photo: Mary Spencer Watson.

1

My Family of Artists: First Impressions of the Isle of Purbeck: My Career is Born

Mary Spencer Watson's father George, the son of a surgeon, was born in 1869. A quiet, unassuming man of great humility, he was an artist by profession specialising in portrait painting. Having studied at Merchant Taylors School and the St John's Wood School of Art he entered the Royal Academy Schools where in 1891 he won a silver medal for drawing, and the Landseer Scholarship in the following year. It was whilst he was still a student that he exhibited his first work at the Royal Academy.

A traditionalist, he believed that in order to paint, one had first to be able to draw. He worked quickly, preferring to finish work on which he had embarked at a single sitting. In 1909 he married Hilda Gardiner the daughter of a Surrey merchant, who was also artistic by nature being a dancer, a mime-artist and a violin player. The couple's only child, Mary, was born in 1913.

'Hilda and Maggie' by George Spencer Watson R.A. – Exhibited Royal Academy, 1912.

Photo: Mary Spencer Watson.

When the Great War broke out in 1914, Mary's father volunteered for the Artists' Rifles, but was considered too old to be enlisted. He spent the next four years as a special constable in Kensington, where he and Hilda had their home, and in his spare time painted in his studio.

Various friends and colleagues of Mary's parents had associations with Dorset's Isle of Purbeck. They included Kerrison Preston, an authority on the poet, artist, and mystic William Blake, who often gave lectures in

Bournemouth; Archibald Russell, patron of the Arts and friend of painter Paul Nash; art historian Kenneth Clark who had associations with Swanage; and Francis and Jessie Newbery. Newbery was Director of the Glasgow School of Art, where Jessie had studied as a pupil. In 1889, they were married. Jessie was subsequently appointed to the staff, where she taught enamelling and mosaic work, and introduced embroidery into the curriculum. In 1918, the couple moved to Corfe Castle in Dorset.

Having learnt of this the Spencer Watsons were encouraged, after the war, to take their holidays in Studland (the name of which derives from the Old English words 'stod' and 'land', meaning 'a tract of land where a herd of horses is kept'), near Swanage. These holidays, which provided essential relaxation from the pressures of London life, continued for seven years.

At that time the only way to reach Studland from Poole and Bournemouth (short of making the 20 mile journey through Wareham and Corfe), was by crossing the narrow stretch of water at the mouth of Poole Harbour in a ferry-boat run by a family called Harvey. So began the family's love of Purbeck.

Mary's mother Hilda studied under the Swiss psychologist Carl Gustav Jung, to whom Mary was introduced in 1921 when she was eight. Jung held his consultations in a garden room at his home by Zurich Lake – he was a great lover of sailing. Mary loved to play in his garden. She remembers him as a large man who loved children. His whole being radiated kindness.

When in that same year they heard of a proposal to build a chain-link ferry across the mouth of Poole Harbour, Mary's parents realised that this would be the end of Studland as they knew it. The place would be over-run! It was therefore necessary for them to retreat further into the Isle of Purbeck.

By a stroke of good fortune Swanage builder George Hardy, who had done work for Hilda at Studland, informed her of a farmer, E.J. Holland, who intended to sell his house, Dunshay Manor (situated 6 miles inland from Studland, and a mile to the north of the village of

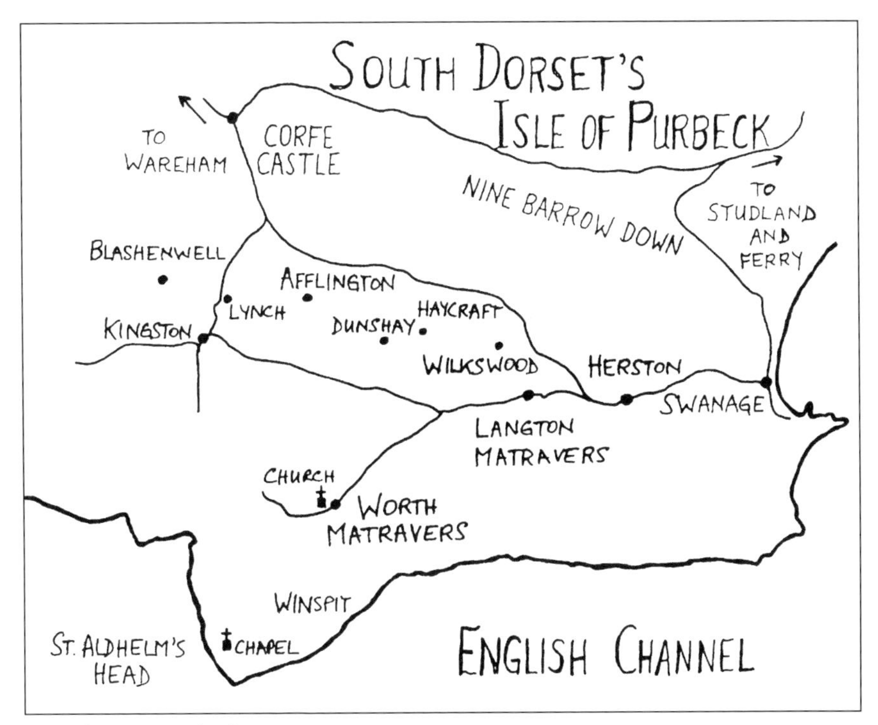

Dunshay in Purbeck.

Worth Matravers – 'Worth'), the property being too large for him to manage. The outcome was that in 1923, the Spencer Watsons purchased Dunshay, together with a few acres of land. Even so, it was necessary for George to keep in touch with his London clients, which meant retaining their house in Kensington. To reach Dunshay from London meant journeying on the train to Corfe Castle, which was a little over 2 miles from their destination.

Hilda now became part of the artistic community which sprung up in Swanage in the early 1920s, and included the Newberys, the English chamber singers David Brynley and Norman Notley, and pioneer studio photographer Helen Muspratt.

'Four loves I found, a woman, a child, a horse and a hound' by George Spencer Watson R.A. 1922. Oil on canvas.
Photo: Mary Spencer Watson.

George found the Purbeck landscape, through which he and his family loved to ride, a great inspiration and many outdoor pictures followed.

Having converted the old dairy-house into a studio with the incorporation of a large north-facing window, George was now free from the constraints of Kensington and portrait painting, and able to indulge his own tastes. For him painting meant becoming emotionally involved in his subject. He loved his family and animals and the Purbeck landscape – these became his favourite choice of subject. He showed no interest in the avant-garde movement, finding abstract paintings cold and clinical.

In his diary he wrote that his faith in art had replaced his faith in Christianity – that Christianity was antagonistic to nature and that nature-worship was a higher ideal. Therefore for him Greek art was on a higher plane than Christian art because the Greeks saw beauty in everything. However this did not deter him from executing murals for a church in Brentwood in Essex, and in 1920 from producing two friezes, the 'Three Wise Kings' and the 'Story of Creation'.

His most famous work, 'The Donkey Ride' was considered picture of the year at the Royal Academy Exhibition of 1919. In 1923 he was elected Associate of the Royal Academy, which gave him the right to exhibit six pictures there every year. Finally in 1932 he was elected to full Membership.

But to return to those first few years at Dunshay. Whilst George painted in his new studio – the converted dairy-house – and his wife Hilda pursued her interests in religion, philosophy and music and developed her dancing, so their daughter Mary began to explore on her own account.

George Spencer Watson painting in his studio, circa 1906.

Photo: Mary Spencer Watson.

When she first came to Dunshay in 1923, Mary was immediately struck by the quietness and slow pace of life compared to London. The sound of rooks chattering in the trees, cows mooing in the fields and cockerels announcing the dawn contrasted greatly with the noise and bustle of the metropolis. They found the manor house to be in excellent repair, and there was also the added luxury of an internal lavatory which had been installed in 1908, when Guy Marsden restored the house with the architect Philip Sturdy.

They set about turning the pond – formed when the old quarry workings filled up with water – into a bathing pool. This was approached by a flight of steps which they built to lead down from a new gateway installed at the far end of the north lawn. The pillars of this gateway had a history to them. The original road to Dunshay ran between the Manor House and the Farm, and people would alight from their carriages before entering through the gateway which was on the southern side of the south lawn.

However, when the new road was constructed and this former gateway blocked off, the columns were used for the new garden gate with finials specially made to match those at the new entrance on the east side. The pool was a delight – they used to bathe before breakfast – it was a lovely place. Sadly it is now overgrown.

Hilda was now able to indulge her passion for Dance-Mime, which she had done in London, and to this end she rented the hall at the Mowlem Institute in Swanage, a Victorian building consisting of library, museum

The old Mowlem Institute, Swanage, with 'Bankers' of stone in foreground.

Photo: David Haysom.

and meeting room with hammer-beam roof of varnished wood. Situated on the sea front, the Institute was presented to the town by John Mowlem, a local quarry boy who went to London, made his fortune and founded the construction company now known as 'Mowlem plc.'

In 1926, Hilda converted the stables into a theatre of her own – designed and built by herself and her husband.

Primary influences were the Diaghilev Ballet with decor by Matisse and Picasso. Children featured in these performances which she produced several times each year.

Above: *Dance-mime theatre – music by Brahms – featuring Hilda and Mary.*

Right: *Dance-mime theatre – music by Monteverdi – 1938.*

Photos: Jessica Sutcliffe.

Hilda preferred to take children with no previous training in ballet or theatre because she found they moved in a more relaxed and natural way. Popular themes were classical mythology and poetry. Photographer Helen Muspratt of Swanage was able to capture and thereby immortalise some of these images, using a process which she had developed called 'solarisation' (whereby her portraits were given a metallic quality by virtue of the prolonged exposure of the film).

൭൭

A child no more than twelve years of age rides her pony up the hill towards Langton village, swinging right towards Worth. She is delivering an order to the quarry for wall stone or 'scars' (waste chippings from worked stone) – as yet there are no telephones hereabouts, the year being 1926.

She hears the sound of horses hooves and reins into the verge to allow the carthorses to pass. The great beasts number twelve, and they are returning from the day's ploughing. She rides along the high road, from which can be seen to her right pastures and isolated farmsteads, whilst to her left the shimmering sea is visible beneath a clear sky.

A pony walking round in a circle catches her eye. The creature is attached to a long pole or 'spack', which turns a round winch – or 'capstan'. Its chain cables are hauling a load of stone up from the quarry below. The capstan is about 6 feet in height and like the spack, is made of elm. It is fitted with a ratchet to prevent the load slipping backwards.

A Purbeck quarry.
Photo: David Haysom.

The capstan is supported on each side by two 'crabstones' set vertically. Before the advent of chains, first produced in the locality by an enterprising blacksmith in Swanage, the early capstans had ropes. The slope on which the stone is hauled up rises at a shallow angle. It is called a 'slide', and the wheeled load-bearing trolley a 'quarr cart'. Prior to this, sledges were used. By rotating the spack, the pony effects the raising of loads of up to 1 ton in weight.

From the slide branched passages fork out at different levels, depending on where the veins of stone are situated, and penetrate up to 100 feet into the rock. The passages are only 3 feet in height. Worked by one man – or a boy as boys were more expendable, not being the primary breadwinners – they are cold and damp. To prevent the roofs caving in, stone pillars are left at intervals.

This is one of the few Purbeck stone quarries remaining in the vicinity, of which there were over 100 in former times. Their gradual demise is because stone has now been discovered near the surface, and open-cast mining is a far more attractive proposition for all concerned.

Curiosity gets the better of her and she draws nearer. A man gives her her friendly wave. This is stonemason Titus Lander. She dismounts and ties her donkey to the branch of a bush. Men are chipping away at the stone with iron chisels and curiously shaped wooden mallets with large rounded heads. From the shape of the finished articles she guesses that it is to be used primarily in the building and ornamentation of houses. Blocks are piled up in 'bankers', awaiting the horse and waggon which will transport them to wherever they might be needed.

A small group of men emerge from the quarry having completed their shift. They are attired in 'moleskins' and shirts and they wear felt hats. They are covered in dust and their hands are calloused, for the winning of stone from the ground is perhaps one of the hardest tasks imaginable. But the men are immensely strong. They are very skilled, yet the work is hazardous, and even more so at the nearby cliff quarries where the stone is transported by boat rather than by waggon, using a three-legged derrick (or 'whim') and capstan to lower it down over the cliff edge.

At the end of the day the entrance will be barred to prevent stray cattle from wandering down the quarry. The pony that obediently turns the capstan will find rest and fodder in the stable; this being adjacent to the 'quarr house' inside which the men can continue to work away at the stone, even in bad weather. The child is Mary Spencer Watson and for her, a lifelong love affair with stone has just begun! This is due in no small part to Titus Lander who, noticing her interest, has the vision and foresight to provide her with the tools and show her how to work the stone.

∾

In 1928 when Mary was sixteen, she enrolled at Bournemouth College to study sculpture under her tutor Mr Ingram, a local man. Two years later she was to be found at the Slade School of Fine Arts in London, being taught the art of modelling in clay by Professor A.H. Gerrard, and learning to draw under draughtsman and etcher Professor Rudolph Schwabe.

Following in the footsteps of her father, Mary went from the Slade to the Royal Academy Schools, returning in the holidays to Dunshay to follow her practice of direct carving in stone: the 1930s was a period when the art of direct carving was being revived by such people as Henry Moore, Jacob Epstein, Barbara Hepworth and Eric Gill. Influenced by the Paris sculptor Ossip Zadkine (1890–1967), her favourite subjects were animals, birds and human beings. Zadkine, born in Belarus of Jewish extraction, attended art school in London and settled in Paris in 1910, where he taught at his Zadkine Schol of Sculpture.

After three years at the Royal Academy Mary transferred to the Central Schools which were oriented more towards crafts, and here was instructed by sculptor John Skeaping who encouraged her in her carvings of animals. Skeaping (1901–1980), son of painter Kenneth Skeaping, studied at various colleges of art before going to Rome to study marble carving. In 1925, he married sculptor Barbara Hepworth. Professor of Sculpture at the Royal Academy Schools, Skeaping was commissioned by pottery manufacturer Wedgwood to design a series of animal figures, which were produced in black basalt.

'The Earth is the Lord's and the fullness thereof' by Mary Spencer Watson, 1990 – Purbeck freestone.
Photo: Mary Spencer Watson.

A sad event occurred on 11 April 1934 with the death of Mary's father George. He was buried at the Church of St James, Piccadilly, which is the chapel for Royal Academicians. Her mother Hilda subsequently organised a Memorial Exhibition to him at the Fine Art Society, of more than 100 of his works. She then relinquished her Kensington home and she and Mary took up permanent residence at Dunshay. In 1937 Mary visited Paris, and Zadkine's studio. It was he who encouraged her to produce large figures on a grand scale.

During the Second World War, the acres of land which Mary's parents had purchased with Dunshay Manor were farmed to assist with the war effort. She helped at the adjacent Downshay Farm, but also found time to teach part-time: first at Clayesmore School and later at Cranborne Chase School and Poole Art School. Friends at this time included Don Potter, who had worked with sculptor and engraver Eric Gill and taught sculpture and pottery at Bryanston School; Elizabeth Muntz, the Canadian sculptor who had worked for Eric Kennington and held the distinction of being the only female member of the Ancient Order of Purbeck Marblers, and Walmsley Lewis, the Weymouth architect, who introduced her to colleagues who in turn gave her commissions to the extent that by 1951 she was able to give up teaching. Her dream was to produce contemporary sculptures to be set amongst mediaeval ecclesiastical buildings, and this derived from the visit she had made to France in 1937. However the greatest influence was to come when she visited Greece in the mid 1950s, and fell in love with the archaic period which preceded the classical.

2

Dunshay Manor in the Parish of Worth Matravers ('Worth')

The road leading to the house is long and winding – a typical English lane. It runs through verdant pastures dotted with ash, oak and sycamore. Its verges, which have been spared the cruel cuts of modern clipping-machines, burgeon forth with buttercups and cow-parsley.

The observant eye would notice depressions and irregularities in the ground alongside, and these give a clue as to the origins of Dunshay, for they are in fact the old workings and spoil-heaps of the marble quarries, and are clearly delineated on the Ordnance Survey map of 1928. As the road winds round towards the house, the quarry-workings lead on through the area adjacent to the northern part of its grounds, which have now become overgrown and wooded.

The seam of the marble, never more than 2 feet in thickness, runs in a narrow band from Peveril Point, a rocky outcrop on the coast at Swanage for 14 miles across country to Lulworth Cove where it has been forced into an up-ended position.

The existence of the marble was known to the Romans, and the little settlements dotted along the valley – which from east to west from Peveril Point are Swanage, Herston, Wilkswood, Quarr, Haycrafts, Dunshay, Afflington, Scoles, Lynch, Lynch West and Blashenwell – most probably originated as mining communities. The Romans used the marble for monumental inscriptions, architectural and decorative veneers, and because of its hardness and durability, household pestles and mortars for grinding. However, it was not until the Normans came that the marble was extensively exploited.

At the end of the road is a courtyard with outbuildings, cottages and a pond where ducks – untroubled by the outside world – create their own cacophony of noise as they squabble amongst themselves! Beyond the impressive wrought-iron front gate, with its stone columns and slender finials are visible the twin gables and protruding porch of the east wing; constructed like the remainder of the house in Purbeck stone with a stone-tiled roof.

The oldest part of Dunshay Manor is the so-called 'long house' (a concept introduced by Norsemen invaders from Scandinavia during the nineth and tenth centuries) in the north-west corner. This is a two-storey Purbeck stone building supported by buttresses, the floor of which is set at a lower level than the remainder of the house. On the ground floor it consists of parlour, kitchen and scullery with a large fireplace. The first floor hall would have been the main room of the house, with a raised stage at one end where the family took their meals.

The furniture of the day – tables, benches and chests – was designed to be functional rather than ornamental. Fireplaces were coming into fashion, with chimneys replacing the open fire which vented straight out through a hole in the roof. The walls would have been hung with tapestries.

The date of this 'long house' is uncertain but there are several clues as to its origin. There are signs of subsidence and evidence of adjacent quarry workings, which indicate that the property may have been built on 'moved ground' – that is discarded rubble from the quarries which subsequently settled.

A lintel above one of the windows is of Purbeck marble, but has the bevelled edge typical of a coffin lid. Perhaps this otherwise valuable object was accidentally cracked in the making, and was utilised here instead of being discarded. It is estimated that as many as 7000 such coffin lids were manufactured in Purbeck in the twelfth century and this may therefore give another indication as to the date of the long house – unless of course the lintel was added some time after its construction, in which case the date of the house would be even earlier.

On the south side of the long house is a lawn set on a raised terrace, which was once the kitchen garden. The footpath between the house and the adjacent Downshay Farm, which has long since been blocked off, is bordered with yew trees on either side. These trees are believed to be about four hundred years old. The more extensive lawn on the north side is bordered beyond by a section of the old quarry. Situated at a lower level and reached by steps leading down, this subsequently filled with water to become a pond. To the west of this pond was an apple orchard (for cider production), which has now reverted to its natural state having been reclaimed by nature.

Leading northwards from the rear of the house are the footings of an old stone wall, half-way along the length of which is a privy with typical stone-tiled roof. The dairy complex consists of dairy-house – where the butter was made – with steps leading up to an overhead loft. A sunken 'pitch-path' leads down to pig sties and calf sheds. No doubt the animals benefited from the constant supply of surplus milk and whey.

Dunshay Manor is of roughly square construction, the present-day building incorporating the ancient living quarters on the north-west side. More recent quarters on the south west side were added in the late sixteenth century. Protruding from the south-western corner is the old cider barn, with loft above and cellars below.

3

Alice Briwere and her Husband, Sir Roger de Pole: Death of Sir Roger

Alice Briwere.

Photo: The Dean.

One day, when Mary Spencer Watson was passing through the city of Salisbury, her mother Hilda purchased a guide book entitled *Notes on the Cathedral Church of St Mary the Blessed Virgin, June 1920,* published by Butler and Tanner Ltd. It was therefore quite by chance that she learned from its pages that a lady called Alice Briwere, wife of Sir Roger de Pole, a Norman knight, was living at Dunshay in the latter part of the twelfth century. The question then arose, did Alice live on the very site of her own house, Dunshay Manor itself?

The proposition might seem improbable, were it not for the fact that other buildings contemporary with Alice's dates still exist in the vicinity, even after the passage of 800 years – for example the nearby parish church of St Nicholas of Myra at Worth Matravers and the chapel at St Aldhelm's Head. Also the mighty castle at Corfe which, had it not been for the attentions of Oliver Cromwell, was durable enough to have survived in reasonable condition to this very day!

So if Alice Briwere did indeed live at Dunshay Manor, then it is most likely that she inhabited the most ancient part of the present building, i.e. the long house. Did she and her husband have the building specially constructed for themselves, or was it previously occupied by another

Norman family who in turn perhaps 'inherited' it from a Saxon family after the Conquest of 1066? This may never be known.

~

Alice's story is as follows. In 1177 – the 23rd year of the reign of King Henry II – she married Sir Roger de Pole (variously spelt 'de Pola' or 'de Poles'), owner of the Manor of Worth, of which Dunshay is a part. (The name 'Worth' derives from the Old English 'Weoro', meaning 'enclosure'. The parish later became known as Worth Matravers.) What were Roger's origins, and how did he come to own Worth? This is the story.

The Manor of Worth is listed in the Domesday Book, when it was held by Roger, Signeur (feudal lord) of Montgomery ('Montgomerie' being a place now known as Sainte Foy de Montgomerie which is situated south of Lisieux in Normandy). Born in about 1030, Roger de Montgomery was related by marriage to Richard I, Duke of Normandy, and had assisted Richard's great grandson Duke William (subsequently known as 'The Conqueror', who was of similar age to himself) in a war with Geoffrey Martel, Count of Anjou. It was Roger who contributed 60 ships to the fleet for William the Conqueror's invasion of England. However he did not take part in the Battle of Hastings, having been left behind to govern Normandy as joint Regent with William's wife the Duchess, whilst the Duke was engaged in his campaign to conquer Southern England.

On 6 December of the following year 1067, Roger de Montgomery came over to England sailing from Dieppe to Winchelsea, where he was rewarded with the earldom of Arundel and Chichester. He was also awarded vast estates in Sussex and Shropshire.

It was in a tract of 'hunting ground in the wilderness' in the hundred of Chirbury (15 miles south west of Shrewsbury, which was owned by three Saxon thanes – 'nobles') that Roger established a Motte and Bailey castle overlooking the strategic ford over the River Severn at Rhydwymen. The surrounding settlement he called 'Montgomery' after his ancestral fief (territory) in Normandy – hence the name 'Montgomeryshire'. In 1071 Roger, who also built castles at Quatford, Shrewsbury, Cardigan and Pembroke, was created Earl of Shrewsbury.

In March 1083 Roger de Montgomery placed his gloved hands on the altar at Shrewsbury and vowed that he would found an abbey of the Benedictine Order on the site of the wooden church. He also founded the priory of St Nicholas at Arundel, and the church of St Mary Magdalene at Quatford in Shropshire, and he restored the seventh century St Milburga's Priory in Much Wenlock. He also made generous gifts to many abbeys in Normandy.

In July 1094 Roger de Montgomery fell ill in the castle at Shrewsbury and entered the Benedictine Abbey, which lay outside the city walls and which he himself had founded along with the castle, to be cared for by the monks. He was to die only three days after entering the Abbey, and was buried there.

About one hundred years later his body was re-interred in the Lady Chapel, behind the high altar and before the altar of the Virgin Mary, and a new effigy was carved. Following the Dissolution of the Monasteries by Henry VIII, the chapel was demolished and the tomb moved to its present site at the east end of the south aisle of the church.

Roger de Montgomery – thirteenth century stone carving.

Photo: Shrewsbury Abbey.

The ownership of Worth duly passed from Roger Montgomery to his son Robert, then via the female line to Robert's daughter Matilda and in turn to her daughter Sibil who married Maurice de Pole. It was Sibil and Maurice's son, Sir Roger de Pole, who married Alice Briwere. When he inherited the Manor of Worth Matravers, which included

Dunshay Manor together with its 476 acre farm, this is where the couple set up home.

ത

In the year 1194, seventeen years after he and his wife had settled at Dunshay, Sir Roger de Pole (whose surname may derive from the fact that he lived not far from the town and harbour of Poole, or 'La Pole' (as was its name in Norman-French) set off for the Crusades.

We may imagine this bearded and moustached knight bidding farewell to his lady and riding off into the distance, not realising that he would see neither her nor his native land again. He wears over his all-enveloping chain mail a surcoat emblazoned with his knight's insignia – a lion rampant argent (in silver) with motto 'Pollet Virtus' – 'Virtue is Powerful'. On top of this he wears a cloak, attached at the shoulder on both sides. A heavy sword hangs from the leather belt around his waist, and as he gives Alice a final wave from the horizon, the sun reflects off the chain mail around his arms and the armoured 'greaves' around his legs and silhouettes him against the sky. And to what purpose does he venture forth?

The Crusades, of which there were to be seven or eight principal ones; and numerous smaller expeditions, originated in 1095 when Pope Urban II appealed on behalf of the Eastern Christians, for support in their struggle against the Turks, who had captured Jerusalem in 1071, and now threatened Constantinople.

In the first Crusade, which for the Christians was the most successful, the Muslims were driven out of the Holy Land which fell to the Crusaders in 1099. The Second Crusade (1147–1149) led by the Kings of France and Germany, failed to stem Turkish incursion into the Holy Land; and in 1187 Jerusalem fell to the Islamic leader Saladin. The Third Crusade in 1189 was led by the English King Richard I (or 'Lionheart'), Frederick I of Germany and Philip II of France. Some of the lost territory was recovered, but not Jerusalem itself. The seaport of Acre, 150 miles to the north of Jerusalem, was successfully besieged by the Crusaders and surrendered after two long years; but such was the discord between the various Christian factions that the Crusader army retreated when almost within sight of its goal!

After another failed assault on Jerusalem, Richard was forced to abandon his dream of recovering the Holy City. He sailed for home on 9 October, 1192, but was shipwrecked off the coast of Istria and finally imprisoned by Duke Leopold of Austria with whom he had previously quarrelled. He eventually returned to England but only after a large ransom had been paid.

We do not know the precise details of how this valiant knight Sir Roger de Pole died. His date of death is given as the '5 or 6 Richard I' – the fifth or sixth year of King Richard's reign – i.e. either 1194 or 5. However as by that time Richard had concluded a treaty with the enemy, we must assume that this date – quoted in the family pedigree – is wrong, or that having been wounded in battle or been taken ill, Sir Roger may have been forced to remain abroad for health reasons, instead of returning home. This, however, seems improbable since the family pedigree states clearly and unequivocally that Sir Roger 'died in the Crusades'.

King Richard himself lost his life in 1199 whilst besieging the Castle of Chalus, in order to punish a baron of the Limousin region of central France for a minor misdemeanour. He was struck on the shoulder by an arrow and the wound proved fatal.

After the death of her husband, Alice became known as Alice Briwere (the name probably deriving from the Norman-French 'de Bruiere', meaning 'from the heathland'). 'Briwere' may have been Alice's maiden name to which on her widowhood she reverted, or alternatively, she may have remarried someone called 'Briwere'.

Some confusion has arisen between this Alice Briwere and another of the same name who was sister of one William Briwere, and wife of Reginald de Mohun of Dunster. The eighteenth-century historian the Reverend Hutchins is adamant that these were two different people. Alice of Dunshay's origins must therefore remain something of a mystery.

One can imagine how Alice must have felt, after losing her husband Roger. Sometimes, when the mist rolled up the valley from the sea, she would imagine that she could see him coming towards her on his great white charger; only to be disappointed when the vision was dispelled by the warm rays of the sun. What was she to do now, with no children to comfort her?

And now to add to Alice's woes came another problem. A distant relative of her late husband, one Robert de Novo Burgo of nearby Bindon Abbey, brought an action in the King's Court against her, 'to recover a moiety (portion) of the vill (village) of Worth, which she then held in dower (a widow's share of her late husband's estate)'.

The lawsuit began in the year 1220 and lingered on with frequent adjournments for five years. Alice argued vehemently that she had been given the land by her late husband Roger on the day he commenced his journey to Jerusalem, and therefore Robert had no claim upon it. Finally, to Alice's relief the Court ruled in her favour. Why had her relative been so anxious to get his hands on this land, the size and value of which to someone of his status appeared quite insignificant? It was her association with Sir William Longspee, Earl of Sarum (Salisbury), to whom she was related by marriage, that would provide a possible answer.

4

Salisbury and its New Cathedral: Alice's Contribution

Alice Briwere was related to Sir William Longspee (Salisbury), by virtue of the fact that her late husband's brother Robert de Pole had married Aubrea who was Sir William's direct descendant.

Sir William, son of King Henry II by the King's mistress Rosamond Clifford ('The Fair Rosamond') had been granted the Earldom of Salisbury on his marriage to Elaide Vitri – known as 'Ela' – the Countess of Sarum. A half-brother of King John (successor to Richard I), whom he served faithfully, Sir William would be a witness to the signing of Magna Carta in 1215. After serving with great valour in the wars with France, the noble Earl was shipwrecked and at one point given up for lost. It was a shock to him on his return, to find that in his absence someone else had made a proposal of marriage to his wife!

There was much excitement in Wiltshire at this time with the prospect of a new cathedral being built at Salisbury. The site of the previous one, at Old Sarum on a hill above the town, was deemed to be unsuitable: being exposed to the winter gales and adjacent to an army fort with which it became embroiled in numerous acrimonious disputes. It was therefore decided to build a new cathedral down in the town itself, and William Longspee was to be heavily involved in its creation.

To begin with, in 1219 a wooden chapel was erected and dedicated in honour of the Blessed Virgin. At Easter the following year the new cathedral was founded with a solemn assembly of bishops and clergy, who walked barefoot in procession singing the Litany. Both Alice Briwere and Sir William were present at the ceremony where Bishop Richard Poore, who was the driving force behind the project, laid foundation stones: one for the Pope, a second for the Archbishop of Canterbury, and a third for himself. Two more stones were laid by Sir William and his wife Ela, and by many others who promised gifts to help with the financing.

Bishop Poore himself donated part of his income to the fabric fund, as did his canons, and a meeting of the Chapter (canons) decreed that were any canon to neglect to pay his regular stipend within fifteen days of the time specified in his agreement, then he was liable to have the corn upon his prebend (share of the revenues of the cathedral) seized and sold in order to pay the sum which he had promised.

Salisbury Cathedral – the west front.
Photo: The Dean.

The building of the cathedral would take forty six years – almost half a century – and the logistics of this colossal undertaking were as follows. 60,000 tons of stone would need to be transported the 12 miles from the mines at Chilmark, which was equivalent to ten cartloads arriving on site each day but not of course during the inclement months of winter. 2800 tons of timber would be required for the roof; this in part was provided by King Henry III (successor to King John), who donated fifty oak trees and granted protection to the ships which would bring them across the sea from Ireland. 400 tons of lead were used to cover the roofs, and glass sufficient to cover three quarters of an acre was required for the windows. The cost of the entire operation was 42,000 marks. But what was Alice's role to be in all this, if any?

The Manor of Dunshay, which Alice inherited on the death of her husband, included the long-abandoned Purbeck marble quarries, and it so happened that no less than 12,000 tons of this material would be required in the construction of Salisbury's great new cathedral.

This was her opportunity. She was sitting not on a gold mine, but on something equally valuable. Now she would be instrumental in reopening the quarries and putting their marble to good use. However, she would seek no payment for the marble, but donate it willingly, for which good deed she would be remembered for posterity.

John Leland, antiquary and library-keeper to King Henry VIII, made a tour of England between 1534 and 1543, and from his notes *Leland's Itinerary* was compiled, and first published in Oxford in nine volumes in 1710. Leland states that according to *The Old Martyrology Book*, 'Alice Bruer (alternative spelling) gave all the marble to this church (Salisbury Cathedral) for xii years'.

൬

The Jurassic period of geological history occurred about 200-150 million years ago. Dinosaurs were abundant, birds were beginning to evolve, and sedimentary limestones were being deposited.

Purbeck marble is actually not a true marble, but oolite, a limestone made up of spherical particles called ooliths. It was laid down in the late Jurassic period by precipitation and accumulation on the bed of an ancient, fresh-water lake. This lake was of vast dimensions and is believed to have occupied an area between the present day Isle of Wight and Dorchester. Intermingled with the ooliths were the shells of the tiny, fresh-water snail Viviparus. Clearly visible to the naked eye, these fossilised shells, together with subtle variations of colour in the limestone, accounts for the attractiveness of Purbeck marble.

Perhaps the most apt description is given by the Reverend Hutchins, who writes: 'At or near Dunshay was formerly dug marble of several colours, blue, red, spotted and grey, but chiefly the latter; all of a coarse sort. The grey is congeries (an aggregation) of shells; vast quantities of it are found in all our ancient churches'.

How, one might ask, did a sedimentary limestone studded with fossilised shells become a substance so exquisite and highly sought after? The answer is that it was geomorphically changed over the ages by the action of heat and pressure into a crystalline substance which, when polished, attains a glorious sheen. Unfortunately however, movements in the earth's crust caused the majority of the marble to be buried beneath hundreds of feet of earth and rock, and fractured it so that even where the seam was visible, its surface appeared like crazy-paving.

ᘓ

For twelve years, marble from the quarries here at Dunshay was hauled overland on wooden sledges drawn by oxen to Corfe Castle where it was 'dressed' (fashioned). The ancient trackways which became etched into the landscape can still be seen to this day. Such was the scale of the industry that according to the Reverend Hutchins the marble chippings which piled up in Corfe's West Street – in those days the village's main thoroughfare – grew to a depth of 10 feet! Corfe soon became the centre of the marble industry and marblers came here from London: amongst them Edmund Corfe, Peter Corfe, Hugo de Corfe and John de Corfe.

From Corfe the marble was taken on in similar fashion to Ower Quay on the southern shores of Poole Harbour. Here it was loaded onto flat-bottomed barges which conveyed it to cargo ships waiting in the South Deep Channel. It was then shipped around the coast to Christchurch Harbour and thence up the River Avon to Harnham Quay from where it was taken overland the further mile or so to the construction site at Salisbury.

Salisbury Cathedral – delicate pillarets of Purbeck marble above west door. Photo: The Dean.

The work involved in extracting the 12,000 tons of Purbeck marble to be used in the construction of Salisbury Cathedral was immense, and there would have been feverish activity along the line of the marble seam from Dunshay towards Haycrafts and Quarr. The quarries were open-cast – as were all those along the valley – with the exception of Afflington, where remains of underground workings have been found.

It has long been thought that the marble was merely extracted at Dunshay before being sent on to Corfe. However the necessary rebuilding of a dilapidated wall in the grounds of Dunshay Manor (which formed the boundary between the old marble quarry and agricultural land) was to put an end to this theory, for within that wall were found a number of highly significant artefacts. Fortunately, this event occurred during Mary Spencer Watson's time there and, being a sculptor herself, she was quick to realise the significance of the findings: otherwise all might well have been lost.

She discovered that the original builders of this wall had used various discarded pieces of Purbeck marble in its construction – notably broken lengths of pillars 12 inches or so in diameter and capitals. Also a long piece with indentations which appeared to be a shard, possibly fractured from a pillar when it was being cut. Had these artefacts not been protected by the wall's outer stones, they would inevitably have crumbled away – Purbeck marble does not take kindly to weathering and is therefore not suitable for exterior work.

Most interesting were some dark, rounded pebble-like stones, each of a size which would fit comfortably into the palm of an adult's hand. Made of iron grit-stone, their purpose was to be used with sand and water to polish the marble. This proves, contrary to popular belief, that dressing and polishing was performed 'on-site' here at the quarry, and not entirely at Corfe.

Extracting the marble from the ground was not difficult because it rested on a bed of shale and could therefore easily be prised out using wedges. Nevertheless, because of previous fracturing by natural forces, it was seldom possible to obtain lengths greater than 10 feet and for this reason the pillars of marble at Salisbury, some of which rise to a height of 60 feet

Mary Spencer Watson with pebble of iron grit-stone used for polishing the marble.
Photo: Mary Spencer Watson.

or so, had to be laid one on top of the other with joins. Also, close inspection reveals that the pillars often have pieces inlaid into them, or consist of two longitudinal sections spliced together. This may indicate that it was not always possible to obtain pieces of even so modest a length as 10 feet.

What is not properly understood even to this day, is how the marble was cut longitudinally and shaped into perfectly straight pillars. Given the fact that marble is an extremely hard substance, it is difficult to imagine a sufficiently sharp and durable tool with which it could be cut.

A circular disc-shaped object, 4 feet or so in diameter with bevelled edge, neat central hole, and square base was also found during the rebuilding of the dilapidated wall, made of Purbeck marble. Various theories have been put forward as to what purpose this might have served; amongst them, the base of a font. However, a visit to the Lady Chapel of Salisbury Cathedral indicates that it was probably intended for the plinth of one of its slim, marble pillars. Did the thirteenth century building surveyor get his calculations wrong and order one plinth too many?

∾

Only five years after the laying of the foundation stones of Salisbury's Cathedral Church of St Mary the Blessed Virgin, the east part was completed, and on Michaelmas Day 1225 the first Mass was sung in the presence of King Henry III who arrived with his Justiciar (Chief-justice), Hubert de Burgh. For the next eight years, after which time he was translated to Durham, Bishop Poore with his clerk of works, Elias de Dereham, pressed on with the building of the cathedral. Henry, who was then only eighteen years old, had already been King for nine years having been crowned in 1216. A great patron of the arts, his life's ambition was to rebuild and enlarge Westminster Abbey.

Purbeck marble was employed in Salisbury's 230 foot long nave to decorate the arcades of its ten bays; the slim pillars being set in scalloped symmetrical hollows around each large stone pier (support). Slimmer shafts still, in clusters or singly, are to be found above in the piers of the arcades of the triforium, and higher still in the clerestory. Marble pillars, pillarets, plinths and capitals also adorn the piers of the aisles and transepts. The total number of such columns, which vary in diameter from a few inches to 18 inches, exceeds 3000.

However, the use of this material was to reach its apotheosis in the Lady Chapel where the arcades are supported by shafts of Purbeck marble of such slender proportions that it would seem impossible that they could support the vaulted stone roof above. Here and there, amongst the capitals of the pillars are to be found carvings of small birds and animals amongst leaves.

It was fortunate that Dunshay lay towards the eastern end of the marble seam, where the marble – which had a reddish tinge – was more durable and weathered better than the bluish, less attractive variety found towards the western end of the outcrop. Also, the pieces to be found at Dunshay were larger than at other sites. However, even this high-grade marble does not wear well when placed on the outside of buildings, tending to lose its sheen and crumble.

Salisbury Cathedral – table in Lady Chapel which tradition has it was used to pay labourers their daily wage of one penny. Photo: The Dean.

5

Alice's Environment, her Death and Commemoration: The Cathedral is Completed: Purbeck Marble and its Legacy

There were three Norman buildings in the vicinity of Dunshay with which Alice would most certainly have been familiar. The first was St Aldhelm's Chapel, named after Aldhelm, born in 640 AD who was the first Bishop of Sherborne and whose name means 'Old Helmet'. The Chapel is situated south of the village of Worth on a headland which represents the southernmost extremity of the Isle of Purbeck.

Chapel of St Aldhelm.

Photo: David Haysom.

The 25ft square structure was built in the latter part of the twelfth century. Behind the altar, on its east wall is its only window, in the shape of a long, thin, tapering slit. A solidly built central pier supports the vaulted roof and graffiti carved into it support the idea that this is a 'Wishing Chapel', where a pin is dropped into a hole in the pier and the person then makes a wish. However, the chapel was primarily a place for religious worship and in the reign of King Henry III was served by a chaplain who was a salaried officer of the Crown. The chapel may also have had a maritime significance – to remind passing sailors of their religion and to encourage them to pray for a safe passage. Within a stone's throw are high and precipitous cliffs, which can be seen from miles out to sea if the weather is clear.

The second was Worth's parish church of Saint Nicholas, who was bishop of the town of Myra in what is now Turkey.

Church of St Nicholas of Myra, before the roofing of the tower in 1868.

Photo: Rector of Worth.

Built in about 1100 AD, its entrance doorway is ornamented with the typical Norman chevron (zig-zag) pattern, above which is an ancient bas-relief, now so worn it is impossible to decipher. The concentric semicircles of the chancel arch are also typically Norman, but this arch may have been imported from elsewhere when the chancel was added in the thirteenth century.

The only piece of Purbeck marble in the church, which was built before the Dunshay quarries were reopened by Alice Briwere, is a slab of stone which forms the triangular arch above a blocked-up doorway.

The third was, of course, William the Conqueror's royal castle at Corfe. Its keep (King's Tower) was built by King Henry I; the 'gloriette' (residential dwelling, including kitchens, great hall, and King's Presence Chamber), the west bailey, and the curtain walls and several of the towers of the outer bailey were built in the reign of King John; and the two mighty gatehouses in the reign of King Henry III. It was upon this mighty fortification, that the security of the entire region ultimately depended.

Alice may have come to Worth's parish church to pray for the safe homecoming of her husband when he was away in the Crusades, and to

Corfe Castle as it may once have looked.

Photo: Mrs Liz Agnew (Corfe Castle Model Village and Gardens).

the chapel of St Aldhelm to make a wish to the same effect, but sadly her prayers and wishes went unanswered. She may also have asked God to find her a new purpose in life after Sir Roger's death; and how joyful she must have been to witness the rise of Salisbury's magnificent new cathedral, built to God's glory, a structure besides which even the mighty castle at Corfe paled into insignificance.

Purbeck marble columns are to be found in many English cathedrals and ecclesiastical buildings, but in particular in the Round Walk of the Temple Church in London. Dedicated on Ascension Day in the year 1240, the building of this church was contemporaneous with that of Salisbury Cathedral and it is possible that Alice Briwere also supplied its marble. Curiously, four centuries later there was to be another link between Dunshay and the Temple Church when, in the year 1661, John Dolling 3rd (the son of John 2nd, owner of Dunshay) was buried there.

The date of Alice Briwere's death is not known, but she was certainly alive, according to the Arundel family pedigree, in the nineth year of the reign of King Henry III which was 1225. Her name is to be found in a fifteenth century manuscript entitled 'Ceremonies and Processions of the Cathedral Church of Salisbury' under the heading 'Bidding (inviting) of the Bedes (prayers)'. Also included are the names of such great personages as King Richard I; King John; King Henry III; Bishop Richard Poore and all the other bishops of the cathedral; and William Longspee Earl of Sarum – for all of whom the people of Salisbury were bound to pray: –

> We shalle make oure prayers to god, besechyng his mercy for alle (all) holy churche (church), that god hit (it) kepe in good estate... For archybysshopes, and bysshopes, and in especial for my lorde the bysshop of this see (episcopal unit) that god kepe in his holy seruise (service)...
>
> For oure souerayne (sovereign) lorde the kyng (and) the queene and alle her children... and alle other lordes, dukes, merkeises (marquises), herles (earles) and barons, and alle tho (those) that haue (have) this land to gouerne(govern)...
>
> We shalle pray and beseche god of his mercy for alle trewe (true) crystyn (christian) soules (souls). In especial for alle bishops soules whos bodyes resteth in this holy place... And for alle soules whos bonys restyth in this churche and churche yard. And alle tho that han (have) yeue (given) to this chirche rentys, vestimentis (vestments), or any other goodes wherby god is the more worshipped in this churche... And the mynysters (ministers) ther of (thereof) better susteyned (sustained). For alle oure Brethern (brothers) and Systren (sisters) soules, all our pareshens (parishioners) soules. And for alle the soules that hath done eny (any) good to this churche.

The prayer then goes on to mention Alice Brewere specifically –

> For the Erles soule of sar (Sir) William Longespe (Longspee), for Iamys (James) soule sumtyme (sometime) lord of Audeleigh

(Audeley), for Iohnys (Johns) soule lord Louel (Lovel), and Thomas soule Monteagu late Erle of Sar (Sarum). For Thomas soule hungerford knyght, for Hubert of Burgh, for Walter soule lord hungerforde, for Alys soule Breuer... (i.e. the soul of Alice Briwere).

Where Alice Briwere found her final resting place is not known. However in 1957 a monumental slab of Purbeck marble was unearthed a quarter of a mile from St Aldhelm's Chapel. It was believed to date from the thirteenth century and underneath was a grave containing a female skeleton. Adjoining this was the foundation of a square, stone building and there was speculation that this was the 'cell' – one-roomed dwelling – of an 'anchoress' – a woman who has withdrawn from the world for religious reasons. Now although one might normally have expected Alice, the widow of a knight, to have had a more dignified burial, who knows?

The thirteenth-century monumental slab – unearthed near St Aldhelm's Chapel, 1957. Photo: Rector of Worth.

The cathedral was built over the course of sixty years. Its length measured externally, would be 449 feet with vaults rising 81 feet above the floor. When the spire was eventually added, its height of 404 feet would exceed the height of the vaults by the astonishing factor of 5. During Bishop Poore's incumbency residences in the Cathedral Close were erected, including his own palace.

Sir William Longspee, Earl of Salisbury, the illegitimate son of King Henry II and half-brother of King John, who had been present at the laying of the foundation stone of the cathedral in 1220, died in 1226. The effigy of him, in chain mail with shield depicting six lions rampant, is made of freestone not Purbeck marble. It is supported on a chest of timber and has the distinction of being the earliest English military effigy. Sir William was also the first person to be buried at the cathedral. After his death his wife Ela founded the nunnery at Lacock in Wiltshire to which she retired.

Effigy of Sir William Longspee, Earl of Salisbury. Photo: The Dean.

In the same year the bodies of the former Bishops Jocelin, Roger, Osmund, and possibly Herman were brought from Old Sarum and interred in the cathedral.

Sir William's eldest son, also William, led the English knights in the Seventh Crusade and died heroically in the assault on Mansoura (in present-day Syria) in 1250. He was buried at Acre, but there is an effigy of him at Salisbury, situated in the nave at the opposite end to the one of his father. Sir William Longspee the younger's effigy is of Purbeck marble, and depicts him as a cross-legged knight with one hand on the hilt of his sword and the other holding his shield up aloft.

By 1248 the cloisters were under construction, and by 1256 the main walls were complete. In 1258, with the completion of the roof, the consecration of the cathedral took place under the then Bishop Bridport, in the presence of King Henry III and his Queen, Eleanor of Provence.

In 1266 the roof was leaded and an exquisite campanile (bell tower) was erected in the north-west corner of the precinct. The Statutes of Bishop Roger de Mortival indicate that this was the year that the whole of the cathedral, including cloisters and chapter house, was completed. The spire, the tallest in England, is thought to have been built between 1280 and 1320.

When in 1240 an effigy of King John was carved for the cathedral of Worcester, the 'effigy industry' became immensely popular. After this no Lord or Lady, Priest or Knight of any note who died could be laid to rest without such a representation of themselves being made. Many marble effigies were carved at Corfe, as were thousands of coffin lids which were also in vogue.

In 1269 King Henry III, realising the enormous value of Purbeck marble, established a group of 49 marblers and 15 marble polishers in London. He was then able to control the sale and distribution of this commodity, as it was becoming highly sought after by cathedrals and churches throughout the land for pillars, tombs and fonts.

In the fifteenth century, however, with the growing popularity of alabaster (a light-coloured translucent form of gypsum), the marble industry gradually declined. In 1551, during the reign of Queen Elizabeth I, the Ancient Order of Purbeck Marblers and Stonecutters received its Charter. Records were kept at Corfe and the marblers met there annually on Shrove Tuesday. According to Hutchins 'their records were unfortunately burnt in the sixteenth century, but copies of a 1551 charter survive'.

The rules of the order were strict. Its chief officer was the Warden, whose job it was to 'adjust differences between the quarrymen and to order the steward if necessary, to summon the whole body to determine a dispute.' Quarries could only be worked by a 'Freeman of the Isle of Purbeck' and to be a freeman one had to be the legitimate son of a freeman. This right passed to a son at the age of twenty-one – up to this time his wages belonged to his parents.

> 'The apprentices appear in court with a penny loaf in one hand and a pot of beer in the other; and upon paying 6s.8d. their names are entered in the register. Upon this they are declared free and at the end of seven years they are empowered to take apprentices... The wife of a Freeman is admitted to her freedom, paying 1s., and if she survives her husband, is entitled to take apprentices and carry on the business.'

The order had a tradition which has persisted long after the demise of the marble trade, whereby after the annual Shrove Tuesday meeting, the members of the company would proceed to kick a football – donated by the most recently married man amongst them – all the way from Corfe to Ower Quay (a distance of 3 miles). Once arrived, they would present the football, together with a pound of pepper to the landowner as payment for the use of the right of way over his land to the Quay from where the marble was traditionally shipped. The landowner reciprocated by presenting the quarrymen with a cake.

Warren Molloy, sculptor and letter-cutter, Corfe Castle, July 2000.

From time to time the marble trade underwent a brief revival, as for example when the new church at nearby Kingston was built in the

1870s, or when the Temple Church in London was rebuilt after the Blitz of 1941.

For the continual restoration work which is necessary in the numerous cathedrals, viz: Exeter, Winchester, Canterbury, Chichester, Lincoln, Beverley, York and Durham, and in those churches where Purbeck marble is to be found, the product is still supplied to this day, from Haysom's Quarry, and from others in the Isle of Purbeck. However, the once thriving marble quarries are now mostly overgrown, and their sites are marked only by solitary farms.

'Koi Carp' (Purbeck Marble) by Warren Molloy.

6

Successors to Alice at Dunshay Manor: Expansion of the Manor House

Alice Briwere held the Manor of Worth in dower (as a gift from her late husband for her own use during her lifetime) and after her death it passed to one Robert Fitzpaine, who was Alice's mother-in-law Sibil's grandson by her second marriage to John Fitzpaine – in other words Robert inherited through the female line.

Worth Manor was owned by the Fitzpaines until the year 1349 when in the absence of an heir, it passed to John Matravers – or 'Maltravers' – hence 'Worth Matravers' – the name by which it is known today. Alianora, granddaughter of John Matravers, married John Fitzalan who was Earl of Arundel and Marshal of England, after which the Manor of Worth reverted to the possession of the Earls of Arundel.

In 1560, the Earl of Arundel – who was in debt to his tailors, victuallers, mercers (dealer in textiles) and money-lenders – put the Manor of Worth up for sale. It was purchased the following year by the trustees of the late Henry Dolling, tenant farmer of Worth, for his eldest son Christopher, who was then probably only a minor. There were 'Dollings' scattered throughout Dorset in 1327, as the Lay Subsidy Tax lists for that year demonstrate. There was also a Count Dolling, a Huguenot, who came from Toulouse and settled in Purbeck in about 1580: so it seems possible that the Dollings were French in origin.

That the Dollings were prosperous is indicated by the fact that in her will, Henry Dolling's widow (whose name is not known) left a full ploughing team of eight oxen, together with harness and plough, and in excess of 120 sheep, 42 cattle and two horses. There were numerous gifts to her friends and servants, including the 'poor people' of the towns of Wareham and Corfe. Her married daughter Elizabeth Browne, received 'two oxen of the youngest sort, one cow called Buckenoll, twenty sheep and one gold ring priced at 13s.4d'. Another daughter, also Elizabeth, received her 'violet gown that the sleeves are open'. A third daughter Marjorie, was left 'half my corn in my Barn and Barton, all of my best apparell, woollen and linen, except 6 of my best kerchies...' – the latter being squares of cloth used to cover the head.

With the purchase of Worth, and its Manor House of Dunshay, the Dollings graduated from being tenant farmers to the ranks of 'new gentry', and as such became Stewards of the local Manor Court. The Court met twice-yearly to amend leases, to ensure that new tenants swore their oath of 'fealty (fidelity) to the Lord of the Manor' and to administer fines to those who failed to maintain their properties, clear their ditches, or allow their animals to stray onto the street or get in amongst the crops.

Christopher Dolling's eldest son was called John. He married Judith and they had five children, the eldest of whom was born in 1611 and was also called John. Christopher Dolling died in 1612 and is buried in Swanage. When John 1st died in 1630 he left his son John 2nd 'his best silver bowl and the feather bed that was in the room over the buttery', in addition to his lands and property. John 1st was buried at Worth. John 2nd married Anne Culliford of Encombe, and the couple had seven children, the eldest of whom, John 3rd, was born in 1638.

In 1641, the year before the English Civil War began, Christopher's grandson John Dolling 2nd was living at Dunshay where his lands were valued at £100; on this he had to pay a Lay Subsidy Tax of £5. The 1664 Hearth Tax records show John 2nd as having 10 chimneys at Dunshay, which would presumably have included not only those of the Manor House, but also those of the outbuildings and labourers' cottages.

In the same year, John Dolling 2nd had been appointed King Charles I's 'Commissioner for the Blandford Division of Dorset' – which included most of the south-eastern part of the county. In this capacity John acted as Assessor to ensure that landowners paid the correct Lay Subsidy Tax which went towards paying for King Charles's war against the Scots. John was clearly back in favour with the King, having ten years earlier been fined the sum of £12.10.0 by His Majesty for failing to attend his coronation! However, the unfortunate John Dolling 2nd could not win because when the Civil War ended, he was fined another £350 by a Parliamentary Committee for Compounding, set up by the House of Commons, for having fought on the side of the King with the rank of major. On the other hand John's cousin Henry, of the same manor and parish, had been fortunate enough to have backed the other – and winning – side, using the ship *Arke* of Poole, of which he owned the greater part, to supply the Parliamentary soldiers in their garrisons at Poole and Wareham.

John Dolling 2nd died in 1663, before his eldest surviving son Robert, born in 1651, had come of age (John 3rd having died in 1661). Like his predecessors, Robert presided over the six-monthly meetings of the Manor Court but his reign as Steward was to be short-lived, for he died suddenly in 1673, at the age of twenty-two. The Manor of Worth then passed to Robert's two sisters: Margaret, who was married to John Pyke, gentleman; and Selina, who married George Duke, esquire, of Southampton.

In 1771, 211 years after the Dolling family had purchased Dunshay Manor and estate, John Pyke the great grandson of Margaret and John, sold his share ('moiety') – portion of the Manor (excluding the farm) to John H. Calcraft, esquire, of Rempstone: a wealthy government servant, Calcraft had bought much property in Purbeck, including the Manor of Wareham! At about the same time, Calcraft also purchased the share which had once belonged to George Duke, and some time after 1682, Downshay Farm also came into Calcraft's hands.

By this time, however, Dunshay Manor was in a state of disrepair, as were the houses round about including Downshay farmhouse, with its labourers' cottages. For the next few years Calcraft decided to let Downshay Farm to a tenant, and the Manor House to a dairyman and his family for whom it would serve as both lodging and dairy house. However, only part of Dunshay Manor was habitable as the north-east wing had collapsed.

Who built the two-storeyed extension on the south-west corner of Dunshay Manor which adjoins the original 'long house'? A clue is that on one side of the lintel – or dripstone – above the ground floor window are carved the initials 'CD', and on the other side the initials 'ED'. They stand for Christopher Dolling, Henry's son, and Elizabeth Dolling (nee Fry) of Mappowder, his wife. This would seem to indicate that it was built by them in the late sixteenth century. The fact that this building shows signs of having undergone a degree of subsidence and has had to be heavily buttressed, suggests that it may have been built on 'moved ground' – that is, on the spoil heaps formed when the marble quarry was excavated.

Above the first floor window appear in red the words 'Cheese Room'. Situated as it is over the kitchen, this room would be warm and dry and therefore the ideal place for the making of cheese. The words were painted in red ochre – the same dye that was used to mark the sheep. They date from the time when there was a tax on windows, and were there to make sure that the assessor did not include this room in the residential part of the house. This dye was to keep its colour amazingly well over the years.

Christopher Dolling's late sixteenth-century extension.

Photo: Mary Spencer Watson.

The most recent part of the house with its twin gables and protruding porch, faces east. Also two-storeyed, its floors and ceilings are at a higher level than in the Christopher Dolling building. The letters 'J D A' are embossed on the rainwater head of the drainpipe on the south side of the porch. These are the initials of John Dolling 2nd and his wife Ann, and the date

1642, indicates that this is when the easterly extension was completed. In keeping with the rest of the house, it is built of Purbeck stone with a stone-tiled roof and mullioned windows. The porch is unusual in that its paving stones are diamond in shape.

The addition of John Dolling 2nd's extension meant the removal of the east-facing windows of Christopher Dolling's original living room. These windows were subsequently taken to the adjacent farmhouse of Downshay Farm and incorporated into the south-facing wall of its living room. The front gate, with its stone piers and delicate cone-shaped finials atop pedestals, was probably constructed at about the same time.

Seventeenth-century extension with porch and twin gables.

Photo: Mary Spencer Watson.

The date of the cider-barn, which extends from the south west corner is unknown. Its cellar contains large stone benches on each side with a drain to act as outlet for the drips from the taps of the barrels. This was a building of importance, it being the custom in former times for the farmer to pay his labourers with cider as part of their wages. What was the cider-orchard, has long since been reclaimed by nature.

The date of the dairy complex on the west side of the house is also uncertain.

Front gate.

Photo: Mary Spencer Watson.

Cider barn. Photo: Mary Spencer Watson.

High up on the north side of the building, and facing the lawn towards what were once the ancient marble quarries, is the stone effigy of a headless man. This was discovered lying in a hedge, during the period of renovation by the Rempstone estate in the early 1900s. Although it is referred to by the local people as 'Old Pyke' – after John Pyke who married John Dolling 2nd's daughter Margaret in 1663 – this figure might equally well be John Dolling 2nd, who extended the house in 1642. Presumably, the sculpture was originally complete because, as far as is known, no-one in real life was ever beheaded at Dunshay!

Pig sties and calf houses. Photo: Mary Spencer Watson.

High up on north wall – 'Old Pyke'.
Photo: Mary Spencer Watson.

7

Another Discovery: Benjamin Jesty and Upbury Farm: The Scourge of Smallpox

In the churchyard at Worth are to be found the gravestones of one Benjamin Jesty 'who departed this life April 16, 1816 aged 79 years' and of his wife Elizabeth, who died eight years later aged eighty-four. Described as an 'upright, honest man' Jesty was, according to the inscription, 'particularly noted for having been the first person (known) that introduced the Cow Pox by Inoculation...' This may come as a surprise to those who had always believed that the Gloucester surgeon Edward Jenner was, so to speak, the first vaccinator.

Also of interest were the words 'Relict of the Late Benj: Jesty of Downshay' inscribed on Elizabeth's tombstone. Was it possible that yet another notable person (i.e. Benjamin Jesty) had also lived at Dunshay? Did the Manor House have yet more secrets to yield up?

Last resting place of Benjamin Jesty and his wife Elizabeth.

Photo: Rector of Worth.

Benjamin Jesty – portrait, by Michael Sharp(e).

Benjamin Jesty was a Dorset farmer, the name 'Jesty' being well known in the farming circles of that county. Many variations of the name exist, including 'Juste', 'Justie', 'Juster' and 'Justy'. He lived in the west of the county, at Yetminster near Yeovil, where he carried out 'an extensive business by sending cattle to the London market'.

Jesty's grandfather John Justy was a butcher at the nearby village of Leigh. When he died in 1700, he left all his goods and chattels (movable possessions) to his wife – 'relict' – Magdalen who was his executrix. Each of his nine children (there had been eleven but the twins, Elizabeth and William, born in 1689 died in infancy) were left one guinea each. The total value of his estate was £350.

Jesty's father – christened Robin but known as Robert – was born in 1679. He became a farmer, married and lived with his wife Edith in a large farmhouse called Winterhayes – once the home of an ancient family of that name – at the nearby hamlet of Rhyme Intrinsica. Robert, who had not been taught to write, signed his will with a cross. Benjamin Jesty, Robert and Edith's seventh child of eight, was born in 1736, In 1770 he married Elizabeth Motley of Long Burton, and the couple set up home as tenants of Upbury Farm, which was situated adjacent to the church in Yetminster.

ᘐ

Upbury Farm was a mediaeval building which was reconstructed in the sixteenth century. It came into being in the following way. At the time of Domesday (King William I's great survey of the lands of England made in 1086) the hundred (division of a county originally supposed to contain about 100 families) of Yetminster was held by Osmunde de Seaz,

The Jestys' house – Upbury Farm, Yetminster, Dorset.

Photo: Tessa Gigg.

nephew of the Conqueror. When the Bishop of Salisbury appointed prebends (canons) to serve in his new cathedral, the hundreds were divided into manors. The manors were then let on long leases and the revenues from them gave the prebends an income.

In the case of Yetminster, there were four such manors 'Episcopi', 'Ecclesiasia', 'Prima' and 'Secunda'. Upbury Farm was in the Manor of Prima, and was probably built by the prebend as his country retreat. The best known of all Yetminster's prebends was William of Wykeham, born in 1324, who was appointed canon of Yetminster Prima in 1361, and went on to be consecrated Bishop of Winchester. The appointment of prebends came to an end in the mid-nineteenth century.

A feature of Upbury Farm's front elevation are two windows with trefoiled heads, fifteenth-century in style, which have been blocked up. They appear not to be in their original position. During the Civil War Oliver Cromwell stabled his horses here. There is a secret passage linking the building to the adjacent church, and it is rumoured that gold plate from the church is buried in the grounds, having been hidden but never retrieved.

∾

The area where the Jesty's lived was frequently ravaged by smallpox, a disease which is believed to have originated in China and which spread to Europe at the time of the Crusades, In the seventeenth century smallpox changed in character from being a relatively minor illness to a dangerous and often fatal one which killed on average, one in ten of the population. Caused by a virus, smallpox was highly contagious, manifesting itself in a sufferer between eight and twenty-one days after he or she had been in contact with someone infected with the disease. Symptoms included aching, vomiting and high fever, violent headache and pains in the back. Spots typically appeared on the third or fourth day, first on the forehead and wrists, before spreading to the whole body. In another four days the spots turned into watery blisters – or 'vesicles' – which then became filled with an offensive-smelling pus. As the fever subsided crusts formed over the pustules which, if sufficiently deep, cause permanent scars or 'pock marks' on healing. Mortality was high, and of those that survived, many were left deaf or blind. Survivors would however, never suffer a repeat attack as the first attack would render them immune to the disease.

In 1713 a paper on the subject of 'Variolation' – the inoculation of a healthy person with material gleaned from the vesicles of someone infected with the disease – was read by Greek physician Dr Emmanuel Timoni to the Royal Society in London. Three years later, after a successful trial of the procedure on prisoners under sentence of death in Newgate prison – who were offered a pardon if they agreed to be 'guinea pigs' – no less important personages than King George I, and Caroline Princess of Wales were willing to risk inoculation. However, the process was known to be extremely hazardous and could actually encourage rather than inhibit the spread of the disease; so it was officially banned under the Vaccination Act of 1840.

People living in rural areas were aware that milkmaids had the singular advantage of never falling prey to smallpox; so not for them the misery

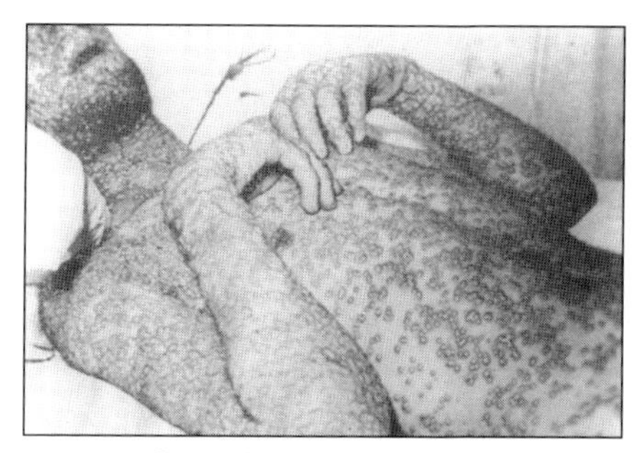

A case of smallpox.
(From The Ship's Medicine Chest*).*

of contracting the dreaded disease and, if they survived, having to live for the rest of their lives with a face pitted with pock marks. Jesty's own milkmaids Ann Motley and Mary Read were typical examples. For this reason milkmaids were the only people who were able to look after the sick, with impunity. In fact Ann attended her brother, and Mary her nephew when they contracted smallpox, but at no risk to themselves.

What was the mechanism by which the milkmaids had developed their immunity? At the time it was believed, correctly as we now know, that it was related to the fact that they had come into contact with cows suffering from cowpox – a not uncommon disease in cattle in those days. In the process of milking the animals, the milkmaids would themselves contract cowpox, from infected matter in the blisters on the udders of the cows which they milked. Cowpox, it should be said, is not a serious disease, either for humans or for cattle, but it did appear to confer upon those who caught it an immunity from smallpox.

In the spring of 1774 – by which time the Jestys had three children – Robert (born 1771), Benjamin Junior (born 1772), and Elizabeth (born in 1773) – the area around Yetminster was smitten by a particularly serious outbreak of the disease. For Jesty, who had been aware of the protective effects of cowpox since he was a boy, and was already immune from smallpox having previously contracted cowpox himself – the choice was obvious. Either he could wait until his vulnerable family became sick, or he could act. He decided to act. He would take the responsibility of immunising his wife and their three children (all of whom were under the age of five) himself!

8

Farmer Jesty Takes a Hand: A Move to Dunshay: Dr Jenner

Living a mile south of Yetminster at Chetnole was a farmer named Elford. When Jesty heard that there was an outbreak of cowpox amongst Mr Elford's cows, he persuaded his wife Elizabeth and the two boys to accompany him to his farm. Their baby daughter was not included as she was considered too young to participate in what was to follow.

Jesty identified a cowpox blister on the udder of one of Mr Elford's cows. Not being equipped with a lancet, he used a stocking (i.e. darning) needle to lance the blister, then pricked some of the matter from it into the forearm of his wife, and into the upper arms of the children! This technique later came to be known as 'vaccination', after 'vacca', the Latin word for 'cow'.

The arms of Jesty's wife Elizabeth, and those of the boys subsequently swelled. They all fell ill with a fever; so much so that Mr Trowbridge of nearby Cerne had to be summoned. 'You have done a bold thing' said the physician, 'but I will get you through it if I can'. Both men would have been aware that had Elizabeth died, Jesty might well have been charged with manslaughter, at the very least! Fortunately however, they made a full recovery.

Jesty's action drew much adverse comment and even 'clamorous reproaches from his neighbours', who objected to him introducing a 'bestial disorder' into a human frame. Jesty however, argued that 'he preferred taking infection from an innocuous animal like a cow', which was 'subject to few disorders', to taking it from the human body, which was 'liable to many and such diseases'. After all, do we not 'already without danger eat the flesh of and blood, drink the milk, and cover ourselves with the skin of this innocuous animal?'

Some idea of the antipathy which Jesty by his action had generated amongst his neighbours may be gleaned from an article which appeared in the journal, *The Lancet* on 13 September, 1862, forty-six years after his death. It was written by a Mr Alfred Haviland, Surgeon to the Bridgwater Infirmary, following a visit by him to the Rose and Crown Inn at Nether Stowey in Somerset, where his attention was drawn to a photograph (taken from a portrait) of 'a fine old English yeoman'. This image was that of Benjamin Jesty, and on the reverse was a copy of Jesty's epitaph, which gave an account of his exploits with inoculation.

On making further enquiries, Mr Haviland learned from a relative of the late Benjamin Jesty, Mrs William May (née Jesty) that 'when the fact became known that he (Jesty) had vaccinated his wife and sons, his friends and neighbours who hitherto had looked up to him with respect on account of his superior intelligence and honourable character, began to regard him as an inhuman brute, who could dare to practice experiments upon his family. The sequel of which would be, as they thought, their metamorphosis into horned beasts. Consequently, the worthy farmer was hooted at, reviled, and pelted whenever he attended the markets in his neighbourhood. He remained, however, undaunted and never failed from this cause to attend to his duties; and the secret of this bold conduct may be traced in his determined chin and nose and firm lips'.

The authorities do not appear to have censored Jesty in any way for his actions because in 1776 we find him serving in the responsible position of overseer to the poor. One of his duties in this regard was to provide parish relief to his cousin William's wife Sarah, who was stricken down with tuberculosis – 'consumption' – whilst pregnant with her fifth child.

The fact that for Jesty, Yetminster had now become a hostile environment may have been a determining factor in his deciding to move away from the area, which is what he and his family did.

In 1797, the Jesty family moved to Dunshay Manor. Their departure from Upbury Farm appears to have been abrupt, as there were complaints from its new tenants about the poor state of sundry gates and fences, which Jesty was ordered to repair.

By this time Elizabeth, who had made a full recovery after being vaccinated by her husband, had borne four more children: Thomas, Sarah, George and Harriet. It is not known whether Jesty inoculated these new members of the family against smallpox, but we can be fairly certain this most independently-minded man would have done so. The fact that he could afford to rent Downshay Farm, a considerably larger concern than the previous farm at Yetminster, indicated that Jesty was continuing to thrive, despite adversity.

Here, Jesty kept mainly sheep, which grazed the lush hills and drank from dew ponds as there were no rivers or streams in the vicinity, and also some cattle.

So what brought the Jestys to Dunshay Manor? A possible explanation is given by the author E. Marjorie Wallace M.A. She pointed out that the Vicar of Worth at that time was the Reverend Morgan Jones, B.A., who in 1793 had also become Rector of Ryme Intrinsica, a village not far from Yetminster where he was to be the incumbent for the next thirty years. As the rector held both livings he would inevitably have travelled frequently between the two parishes, and it was possibly through him that Benjamin Jesty heard about a certain Mr Calcraft of Rempstone, the owner of Dunshay who was seeking a new tenant.

෴

In the meantime the Gloucester physician, Dr Edward Jenner was pursuing his own agenda to eradicate smallpox. He himself had been inoculated with smallpox material in 1760 and had become seriously ill as a result.

Whereas Jesty's vaccination had been cow-to-human, Dr Jenner's was now to be the first human-to-human vaccination, for in 1796 (twenty-two years after Jesty's vaccination of his own family), Jenner took cowpox matter from the hand of a dairymaid called Sarah Nelmes and scratched it into the arm of James Phipps, a boy of eight years old.

Jenner went on to prove the success of this technique, when he subsequently injected smallpox matter into the boy, who failed to contract the disease. The medical establishment now embraced Dr Jenner's ideas and the technique of vaccination swiftly became acceptable throughout the land. When in 1802 Jenner petitioned the House of Commons to reward him for his 'discovery', a committee was set up to discuss the matter. The question to be answered – was Jenner the first to make the discovery?

In attempting to reach a conclusion, the committee studied a letter from a Dr Pearson of the Smallpox Hospital in London who had once worked with Jenner before the two men fell out. Pearson had heard of the exploits of Benjamin Jesty and, motivated perhaps by feelings of antagonism towards Dr Jenner, he was anxious to draw Jesty's pioneering work in the field of vaccination to its attention.

The matter was concluded when William Pitt the Prime Minister stood up in the House of Commons to say that Dr Jenner 'had made the discovery and had given it liberally to the world'. Jenner was awarded £10,000, followed by a further £20,000 in July 1807. In 1821, Jenner had the further honour of being appointed Physician Extraordinary to King George IV. This however, was not the end of the story.

9

Dr Bell: London

Reverend Dr Andrew Bell, D.D.

Photo: Rector of Swanage.

In 1801 the Reverend Dr Andrew Bell, D.D. was appointed Rector of Swanage and Worth. He had recently returned from India, having made a fortune from judicious investments, whilst at the same time holding the post of Superintendent of the newly-opened Madras Asylum for male orphans.

It was while he was in India that Dr Bell invented his 'Madras System' of teaching, whereby in addition to formal instruction, his pupils were encouraged to help educate one another.

When he arrived in Swanage there was little in the way of education, child labour being the rule, rather than the exception. However, within six years of the energetic Dr Bell's arrival, no less than 13 day schools and three Sunday Schools had been opened in the parish. His schools also taught straw-plaiting, which provided the pupils with the prospect of an alternative lifestyle to labouring in the fields or quarries. Now, they were taught to make baskets, hats and bonnets for which there was a ready market.

Dr Bell was aware of the work of Dr Jenner, 'that great benefactor of the human race', thanks to whose 'ability, industry, and well-directed exertions' the practice of inoculation had been 'diffused over the globe', and he now set about introducing the practice to his parishioners and others in the neighbourhood of the Isle of Purbeck; upwards of three hundred of whom were vaccinated. However, Dr Bell was astonished to discover that there were still 'some who questioned the efficacy of vaccination as a preventive of the Small Pox', and that some parents still declined 'to submit their children to this simple operation'.

When Jesty got to hear of Dr Bell's work, he was anxious to draw the doctor's attention to his own feat of inoculation back in 1774; and also to suggest that he, Jesty (like Dr Jenner) might be entitled to some reward on account of it. This knowledge prompted Dr Bell in 1803, to describe in detail the incident at Chetnole to the newly created 'Jennerian Society of London' (which had been established by Jenner in that same year).

The result was that the following year, Jesty was invited by the Society to London. He refused the invitation however, 'being apprehensive of an attack of gout', but when the Secretary of the Society, Will Sancho approached him a second time, he accepted. You are 'to come to town at your own convenience', said Sancho, 'but as soon as possible, to stay not longer than five days, unless you desire it, for the purpose of taking your portrait as the earliest inoculator for Cow Pock, at the expense of the institution'. Jesty would receive 15 guineas for his expenses.

For his visit to London in the summer of 1805, Jesty was accompanied by his eldest son Robert, who was then aged thirty-four. The Reverend J.M. Colson of Swanage had 'a perfect recollection of old Jesty coming to our house at Corfe... to borrow of my father a pair of saddle-bags to contain his clean shirts when he was going to London to give evidence on his discovery of vaccination'. However, as saddle-bags were regarded as 'a thing of bygone ages', Jesty was 'supplied with a portmanteau as a more convenient vehicle'.

According to Dr Bell, in London the pair 'met with great attention from the members of the society, who were much amused with Jesty's manners and appearance. Before he left home, his family tried to induce him to attire himself somewhat more fashionably, but without effect. He (Jesty) did not see, he said why he should dress better in

London than in the country; and accordingly wore his usual dress, which was peculiarly old-fashioned'. 'In order to prove their statement', Dr Bell continued, 'Mr Robert Jesty willingly consented to be inoculated for the Small Pox, and his father for the Cow Pock; but neither took effect'. In other words, they had immunity to these diseases. 'Mr Jesty was presented with a pair of very handsome gold-mounted lancets, and his portrait was also taken (painted) by Mr (Michael) Sharpe' says Dr Bell, 'but he proved an impatient sitter, and could only be kept quiet by Mrs Sharpe's playing to him on the piano.'

A statement, drawn up and signed by members of the Jennerian Society read as follows: 'The remarkably vigorous health of Mr Jesty's wife and two sons, now thirty-one years subsequent to the Cow Pox, and his own healthy appearance, at this time seventy years of age, afford a singular proof of the harmlessness of that affection (i.e. vaccination)'.

In the opinion of the members, Jesty's 'exemption from the prevailing popular prejudices', and 'disregard of the clamorous reproaches of his neighbours, will entitle him to the respect of the public for his superior strength of mind...'. Also, 'his conduct in again furnishing such decisive proofs of the permanent anti-variolous efficacy of the Cow Pock... by submitting to inoculation, justly claims at least the gratitude of the country'. Mr Sharpe's portrait of Jesty would henceforward be 'preserved at the original Vaccine Pock Institution'.

An excellent description of the portrait is given by surgeon Mr Alfred Haviland, who refers to Jesty as 'a good specimen of the fine old English yeoman, dressed in knee breeches, extensive double-breasted waistcoat, and no small amount of broadcloth. He was represented sitting in an easy chair, under the shelter of some wide-spreading tree, with his stick and broad-brimmed hat in his left hand; his ample frame was surmounted by a remarkably good head, with a countenance which at once betokened firmness and superior intelligence'.

The Reverend Colson recorded that on Jesty's return, 'he gave a very unfavourable report of the metropolis; but, per contra, said there was one great comfort there indeed – viz., that he could be shaved every day, instead of wearing his beard from Saturday to Saturday, on which day alone – when he rode into Wareham market – was he relieved of that encumbrance'. The following year, Jesty wrote to Dr Pearson of the Vaccine Pock Institute to ask if he might be entitled to any pecuniary reward, for his actions thirty-two years previously. None however, was forthcoming.

In the church at Worth is a memorial to Mary Abigail Brown, who was born in the parish in 1830, and died in Poole in 1901. Described as a person 'ever ready to do good to others' and 'exemplary in all the duties of life', she was 'personally inoculated for cow-pox by Benjamin Jesty...'. This shows that Jesty, far from being deterred from doing what he knew not only to be right but also to be efficacious, continued his practice of vaccination, and even extended it to those outside his own family.

Jesty would have been gratified that his son Benjamin, followed his example and himself became an enthusiastic inoculator. In 1809 for example, he is said to have performed the operation on great numbers of people, and also to have kept a register of their names, and a record of each one's progress thereafter.

In 1806 Dr Bell preached two sermons in a single day on the virtues of vaccination. In his time he vaccinated no less than 658 people of all ages, not one of whom subsequently contracted smallpox. He also encouraged schoolteachers to carry the practice to adjacent parishes, having first personally instructed them in the technique.

Dr Bell left Swanage in 1809 to become Master of Sherburn Hospital in Durham, where he could concentrate on the education of children. Meanwhile Scrap Street, in Herston, Swanage, was renamed Bell Street in his honour.

10

Death of Jesty: Fate of his Family: In the Light of Present Knowledge: Latter-day Owners of Dunshay: Dunshay is Let

Benjamin Jesty died on April 16, 1816 at the age of seventy-nine. In the words of Mr Haviland, 'After living to see another (that is Dr Jenner) enriched and immortalised for carrying out the same principles for which he had been stoned (metaphorically speaking? – or perhaps in reality) thirty years before, he died of apoplexy (a stroke)'.

Worth Matravers village (as it looked fifty years after the death of Jesty, after the restoration of the church and roofing of the tower).

Photo: David Haysom.

Jesty was buried in the church-yard at Worth. After his death, his wife Elizabeth and son, young Benjamin, immediately left Dunshay and went to live at Woolbridge (now known as Wool), a village 5 miles to the east of Wareham. Elizabeth lived on for another eight.

On Jesty's tombstone it states that he was the first person known to have introduced the cow pox by inoculation. There had been reports of others having done so before him but his was the first case to be fully documented (by a man whose honesty is borne out by his having been appointed Land Tax Assessor and Collector, and whose intelligence by the fact that he possessed a modest library of books). His action could also be corroborated by those present at the time.

From his will it is apparent that Jesty died a comparatively wealthy man. His eldest son Robert received the sum of ten pounds and 'my household tenement estate, land hereditaments (i.e. land to be inherited) and premises situate(d) at Yetminster' (indicating that Jesty also also owned property in his old home district). His second son Benjamin (and one Joseph Willis of Norden on the Isle of Purbeck) received the sum of two hundred pounds in trust. The dividends from this trust were to be payable both to them, and to his widow Elizabeth for the term of her natural life. Elizabeth was also left 'a proportinall part of my household goods, furniture and linen as will be sufficient for her own use', and the sum of ten pounds per year for life. The 'residue and remainder' of his 'household goods, furniture, linen, plate, books, stock, crop farming utensils, implements in husbandry, monies and securities for money' he also gave and bequeathed to Benjamin junior.

His third son Thomas, who appears to have fared less well than his siblings, received the sum of one hundred and forty pounds. His fourth son George, and his daughters Elizabeth, Sarah and Harriet received twelve hundred pounds apiece – a very considerable sum indeed for the times – and George, Sarah and Harriet also each received one feather bed.

The will was detailed and meticulous, Jesty requesting that contingencies such as what was to happen in the event of the death of one of his children were to be taken into consideration. He also requested that Benjamin should provide a home for his widow, which he did.

The portrait of Jesty, which had been painted in London, passed from Dr George Pearson, founder of the Original Vaccine Pock Institute, to Pearson's son-in-law who gave it to Edith, the widow of Benjamin's son Robert. It then passed to Edith's grandson, whose family emigrated to South Africa, and today its whereabouts is unknown. However, there is a copy of the portrait in the Dorchester County Museum.

∾

Jesty's eldest son Robert married Edith Cave of Fordington. He farmed at Melbury Bubb and in 1798 is to be found in the list of Volunteer Rangers under Captain Meggs. However in 1832 he was living at Clutton near Bristol, where in 1832 he found himself sharing a coach with the surgeon and geologist Gideon Mantell. Mantell described Robert as 'a shrewd and intelligent farmer' who 'amused us much with his droll remarks'. They had three children.

The second son Benjamin, who farmed at Woodstreet Farm, Wool, where he lived with his widowed mother, married Ann Jennings of Evershot. They also moved to Melbury Bubb, where he continued farming. In 1802 he appears in the records of the Dorset Militia.

When Elizabeth died on January 8, 1824 at the age of eighty-four years, her body was taken back to Worth to be buried in the churchyard alongside her husband.

The third son Thomas married Sarah Cull and became a tenant farmer at Melbury Osmond and later at Batcombe. The youngest son George, described as a 'gentleman', married Sarah Hart and farmed first at Sturminster Marshall and latterly at Druce near Puddletown. The couple had nine children. A link with the present time is that Druce Farm was chosen as the location for Farmer Boldwood's house in the film based on Thomas Hardy's story, *Far From the Madding Crowd*, starring Julie Christie and Alan Bates.

The two elder daughters Betty and Sarah did not marry and the 1841 census shows them sharing house with their brother George. Harriett, the youngest daughter, married William Bennet of East Orchard in 1813, and had one son.

~

No direct descendants of Benjamin Jesty have been discovered, although many claim that distinction. There are however, known descendants from Benjamin's brother William, who was born in 1734.

~

The mechanism by which the cow pox conferred its immunity is now understood, though Jesty, Dr Bell and the learned gentlemen in London who were experts in the field could not have been aware of this in their time, given the limited state of scientific knowledge at the beginning of the nineteenth century.

When foreign material such as cowpox matter is introduced into the human body, the body responds by making 'antibodies' (protein molecules). These antibodies then lock onto it and neutralise it. Now because the cowpox and smallpox viruses have similar structures and the body cannot differentiate between the two, the antibodies made in response to cowpox are equally effective in combating smallpox.

So why was this process not effective when a previously unvaccinated person was infected by smallpox? The answer is that smallpox was such a powerful virus that it overwhelmed the body before the antibodies could be effective. The person previously inoculated with cowpox however, is able to make his or her antibodies that much faster, and in this way effectively to combat the disease. Also, in such a person some antibodies will have remained in the system from the vaccination, and will therefore be instantly available for the counter attack.

In the twentieth century the World Health Organisation's programme of intensive vaccination (which included the surveillance of ships and aircraft to prevent the disease from spreading) led in the year 1979 to an announcement in Geneva by the Global Commission for the Certification of Smallpox Eradication, that this dreadful disease had now been eradicated from the face of the Earth.

How are Farmer Jesty's actions viewed today? Was he an irresponsible person willing to gamble with the lives of his family, or a strong minded man who did his duty as he saw it and stuck to his guns, as it were, no matter what public opprobrium was heaped upon him afterwards? The answer is undoubtedly the latter. Sad to relate, Dr Jenner never in his lifetime acknowledged the truth that Benjamin Jesty, and not he, had been the first vaccinator.

Outside the main gateway of Dunshay Manor is a block of stone with concentric grooves and one long groove etched in its surface. It may once have been the base of a cider press or a cheese press, but was subsequently used as a mounting block. One must admire Jesty who, at the age of seventy, clambered up onto his horse – probably using this very block – to begin the 120 mile ride from Dunshay to the Vaccine Pock Institute in London, which he and his son Robert accomplished on roads that were little more than rough tracks, a journey which would have taken them several days.

෴

To be found on the rainwater head on the downpipe on the north side of the front porch of Dunshay Manor are the letters 'M G M' and the date '1906'. These are the initials of (Captain) Guy M. Marston, the inheritor of the Calcraft Estate. It was the Captain who restored Dunshay Manor's dilapidated north-east wing and made it habitable once again.

Marston let the Manor House to a succession of farmers until 1919 – the year following the end of the Great War – when he sold off a considerable part of the estate. The remainder, which included Dunshay Manor, passed in turn to his nephew Douglas C. Ryder of Rempstone Hall. Ryder subsequently sold Dunshay Manor to farmer E.J. Holland, from whom it was purchased by Mary Spencer Watson's father George in 1923.

The mounting block presumably used by Jesty when he set off on horseback for London.

Photo: Mary Spencer Watson.

11

Lucy Kemp-Welch, R.I., R.O.I., R.B.A., R.C.A.

Prior to the Spencer Watsons coming to Dunshay in 1923, yet another colourful personality arrived on the scene, and spent her summer holidays here in the early 1920s, namely Lucy Kemp Welch.

Lucy Kemp Welch.

Photo: By kind permission of David Messum Gallery, London W1.

Lucy was born on 20 June, 1869, in the fashionable town of Bournemouth (founded by Captain Lewis Tregonwell, who built a house there in 1810, and subsequently known as the place where those suffering from tuberculosis – the scourge of Victorian England – came to convalesce and take the sea air). Her sister Edith was born the following year, and the two girls were educated by a series of tutors.

It was during the time of Farmer Holland's ownership of Dunshay that Lucy (responding presumably to an advertisement in the newspaper), used to come over from Bournemouth and spend her summer holidays there as a paying guest. Why? To paint, of course: for this is how she made her name.

Her childhood was overshadowed by the fact that in 1877 when she was eight, her father Edwin, partner in a firm of Poole solicitors, was diagnosed with pulmonary tuberculosis. In that same year, he purchased a first edition of the book *Black Beauty* by Anna Sewell (first published in 1877). Anna came from a family of devout Quakers. She too suffered from tuberculosis, and at the time of writing her only novel – but one which would make her famous – she had been confined to the house for a period of six years. She wrote it from her sofa, at intervals, according to whether she could muster up the strength required; her mother having to transcribe the words to make them more legible.

In *Black Beauty*, where it is the horse who 'tells the story', Anna demonstrates her enormous insight – her aim being to promote the idea of kindness, sympathy, and understanding in the treatment of horses. The process of 'breaking in' is described, whereby when the harness is put on, the horse, 'may neither jump for joy nor lie down for weariness'. There are numerous references to cruel and unnecessary whippings and floggings, and the use of sharp bits which hurt the tongue and jaw. The book describes how horses can be frightened by the sound of railway locomotives; ignorant people, who do not realise that when a horse goes lame, it may be because of a stone in the shoe; those who punish horses when they shy, when in fact the horse only does this because he is frightened. Black Beauty himself was once so 'overloaded' (i.e. required to haul excessively heavy loads), that he collapsed between the shafts of the cab he was pulling. However, not all is doom and gloom, for Black Beauty, who had several owners in the course of his life, was quick to extol the virtues of a good master.

Anna Sewell died early in 1878, having lived only just long enough to witness the tremendous success of her book. As for Lucy Kemp-Welch, *Black Beauty* made a lasting impression on her, for she was able to identify with Anna's tremendous empathy for what were to both of them, noble and lovable creatures.

Lucy and her sister were educated privately at home by various tutors, and then at Faringdon House, a private school in the town. They had several pets including a terrier named 'Podger'.

Lucy's interest in horses commenced at an early age. She had heard how the artist George Stubbs had buried horses (presumably deceased ones!) and later exhumed their bodies so as to study their skeletons: so she and her friends did the same with dead mice and birds! At the age of fourteen her mother sent her as a birthday treat to a friend of the family, Mr Goodall – a veterinary surgeon in charge of the Hospital for Sick Horses at nearby Christchurch. Goodall not only taught her about the anatomy of horses, but also showed her drawings which he had made when as a student he had performed dissections on the animals. In 1888, Lucy's father died after a long illness.

Having been told by an aunt of theirs about an art school run by Hubert von Herkomer at Bushey in Hertfordshire, Lucy and Edith applied, and were accepted. Born in Bavaria in 1849, Herkomer became Slade Professor of Art in 1885 (and in 1907 he would receive a knighthood). Lucy's entrance to his school was delayed however, owing to the illness and subsequent death of her mother in February 1892. Herkomer was scrupulously fair in allocating places at his school in equal numbers to both sexes. He also offered four annual scholarships: two for males and two for females.

Herkomer's school placed great emphasis on the study of the human form from the life. However, when one day Lucy espied 'a long procession of horses of all sorts and types going up the muddy road, no doubt to Barnet Fair a few miles off... shepherded and driven by wild-looking gypsy men on horse-back...', she could not resist making a sketch of the scene. The final result was an oil on canvas (the canvas being 8ft x 4ft in size) entitled 'Gypsy Horse Drovers'. The painting dwarfed its creator Lucy, who was herself short in stature. This, by a student as yet still only in the Preliminary Class, so impressed Herkomer that he advised Lucy to send the work to the Royal Academy, where it was purchased by Sir Frederick Harris for the sum of £60 even before the opening of the Academy's exhibition where

'Gipsy Horses/Autumn Gold'.

Photo: By kind permission of David Messum Gallery, London W1.

it was displayed! With this success behind her, Lucy was able to take commissions for 'horse paintings' such as 'Summer Drought in the New Forest', and 'In the Marshes' – the New Forest being one of her favourite summer haunts.

A visit to the beach at Parkstone, Poole, resulted in 'Foam Horses', where the animals appear on the crest of the waves. This was exhibited at the R.A. in 1896. She would return to the same place in 1899 to paint the equally spectacular 'Horses Bathing in the Sea'.

For another work of hers entitled 'Colt Hunting in the New Forest', Lucy was obliged to ride deep into the Forest: she to gain inspiration, and the 'colt hunters' to catch and brand the colts (for identification purposes). The final canvas measured no less than 10ft x 5ft, and had to be transported by horse and cart in a huge wooden box. It was hung at the Royal Academy in 1897 and purchased for the nation by the Chantrey Bequest (Sir Francis Chantrey, sculptor, born 1781, having provided money to the Royal Academy in his will for the purchase for the nation of paintings and sculpture executed in Britain by artists living or recently deceased; the collection to be put on permanent display at the Tate Gallery). This was one of four paintings chosen for the Victorian Era Exhibition at Earl's Court, celebrating Queen Victoria's Diamond Jubilee. Lucy was annoyed, however, that it was placed in the Women's Section, as it was her belief that in Art, men and women should not be separated. Lucy now purchased a house at Bushey. Commissions arrived from publishers J.M. Dent and Ward Lock for her to illustrate their books. She joined the local church, and in her spare time played for the hockey team and went bicycling.

In July 1899, she was at Poole painting cavalry horses having their annual 'holiday', the work being entitled 'Horses Bathing in the Sea'. October saw the outbreak of the Boer War, which gave Lucy further scope for horse paintings with such works as 'In Sight: Lord Dundonald's Dash on Ladysmith' and 'Sons of the City', depicting the City of London (mounted) Imperial Volunteers. Professor Herkomer however, discouraged Lucy from embarking on any more of these so called 'narrative paintings'. She should concentrate on the horse, rather than on 'Homo' (Sapiens). Lucy accordingly proceeded to paint horses in all their numerous roles – ploughing, hauling timber, harvesting, pulling waggons and carts, as well as relaxing on the downs or in the forests. Although beautifully executed, with colour and dynamism, these paintings are in no way sentimental. Lucy was acutely aware that the life of the horse was one of unremitting toil and hardship; especially in the cruel months of winter. With the beginning of a new century, she turned her attention to the mare and her foal: one such illustration 'My Mother and I', appearing as an illustration in the book *Black Beauty*. In this, she showed great insight into the immense tenderness which the creatures had for one another.

As for her own life, she remained single: perhaps influenced by her observation that once her female students married and had families, that was usually the end of their painting careers. The year 1903 saw her once more in the New Forest, and also in Scotland painting 'Above the Dee', featuring a Shetland mare and her foal.

In 1902, Lucy was elected to the Royal Society of British Artists – thus becoming one of their first lady members. By now she had added seagulls, dogs, and ducks to her repertoire of paintings! In 1904, Professor Herkomer resigned as president of the art school which gave Lucy the opportunity to purchase it herself. In January 1905, she duly re-opened it as 'The Bushey School of Painting'.

In 1907 she was on Exmoor, painting 'For Life' – which depicted the hunting of a stag. For this, she brought two horses down from Bushey by train. One was 'Folly'; the other, 'Black Prince' (which had been presented to army officer Robert Baden-Powell by the people of Australia after the siege of Mafeking), who was now serving out his days as a 'model' at her school. On 20 June, 1908 (the year Baden-Powell founded the Boy Scout Movement), which was her birthday, Lucy was invited to the Royal Garden Party at Buckingham Palace.

Lucy was unable to make a success of her Bushey School of Painting and in 1911 the buildings were sold back to Professor Herkomer and demolished. Lucy relocated to Rudolph Road and renamed her school – now smaller in size – 'The Kemp-Welch School'.

In 1913, Lucy, encouraged by artist Alfred Munnings, was instrumental in the creation of the Society of Animal Painters, of which she would become the first president. Although she could hardly be described as a militant supporter of the suffragist movement – whose aim was to achieve votes for women – nevertheless it was a tenet of hers that men and women painters should be treated as equals; and the newly formed Society would permit them to be so.

'Forward to Victory – Enlist Now'.

March 1914 marked the death of Lucy's mentor Professor Herkomer, and on 4 August, war was declared on Germany. To Lucy's relief, Black Prince was considered too old for wartime duties. By 1917, the British Army would employ in excess of 860,000 of these animals, of which losses in action – though mainly through disease and privation – would amount to in excess of 250,000. When the Parliamentary Recruiting Committee approached Lucy with a view to her making a poster for them, she duly obliged. Black Prince would model for the charger, and Rowland Wheelwright, formerly assistant master at her school, would model for the horseman.

Lucy enrolled for a course in first aid, but to her intense disappointment was refused permission to serve in France. However, she was allowed to paint the field gun crews practising on Salisbury Plain: the result being the dramatic scene 'Forward the Guns'.

In 1915, Lucy was asked to illustrate a new edition of *Black Beauty* by publisher J.M. Dent, the book which she had so enjoyed as a child. Her model for the story was Baden-Powell's horse, Black Prince.

'She Chose Me for Her Horse'. Black Beauty, *by Anna Sewell.*
(Frontispiece, J. M. Dent's 1915 edition)

In 1919, Lucy commenced a commission entitled 'Women's Work in the Great War', depicting women attired in various uniforms according the respective wartime roles which they had played. It was installed in the Royal Exchange, and unveiled by Princess Mary on 28 April, 1924. In the same year, Lucy was asked to record for the Imperial War Museum, scenes from the Ladies' Army Remount Depot at Russley Park in Wiltshire, prior to its disbandment.

1919 found Lucy in Cornwall, where she had gone with her sister Edith, who was convalescing after an operation. This visit inspired such exuberant works as 'The Glory of the Setting Sun', and 'The Sapphire Sea', reflecting wonderful light and colour.

It was in the early 1920s that Lucy began the first of several summer visits to Dorset's Isle of Purbeck, making Dunshay Manor her base of operations. Her painting, 'On the Purbeck Hills' was purchased by a Canadian, Philip Dennison, who had fought on the Allied side during the Great War.

'On the Purbeck Hills'.
Photo: Philip Dennison.

~

Although Lucy had opportunities to paint thoroughbred Arab horses, her preference, as she made clear, was to paint what she called the 'natural type' that is, those which were 'fashioned by nature and not by man – full of faults, variable, beautiful, and lovable beyond words.' Doubtless she could also have made an excellent living painting the well-to-do riding around in their carriages, but this was of little interest to her. The horse, rather than mankind must, as far as she was concerned, always be the primary object of the painting.

The magnificently evocative 'Launching the Lifeboat' depicts horses struggling into a foaming sea; 'Polo – The Great Game', is self explanatory; and 'Elephants and the Big Top' reflects the time from the summer of 1926 when Lucy travelled with the circus to take advantage of opportunities for further colourful and dynamic works. She admired gypsies, and took every opportunity to paint them and their caravans; envying them the slow pace of their lives, and realising that their culture and customs were in danger of being suffocated by the modern world.

Perhaps Lucy's greatest contribution to her art, apart from the joy which her paintings have given to countless people, whether horse lovers or not, is the way she has elevated the horse to a higher plane. Since Lucy, we see them not simply as mechanical 'tractors', but as living, breathing, sentient creatures, able to offer love, faithfulness, and devotion, not only to their fellows, but also to human beings, whose lives so often depended upon them. Lucy Kemp-Welch died in 1958, at the age of eighty-nine.

12

Leslie Everett Baynes, A.F.R.Ae.S.: The Great War: Between the Wars: Gliders

When, in 1953, Mary Spencer Watson of Dunshay placed an advertisement in *Horse and Hound* for a tenant, she had no idea that this would lead to her meeting a genius of the aeronautical world whose work and ideas would revolutionise the concept of flight. The circumstances were these: her mother Hilda had just died, and she (Mary) was at that time heavily involved in architectural sculpture; as a result of which she was seldom at Dunshay. It therefore seemed sensible to advertise for a tenant, which she did: thinking to herself that with stabling and grazing available for horses, it would be ideal for a family.

Leslie Baynes was an aircraft designer with his own business at Ascot. He and his wife Margot had four children – Jane, Susie, Nigel, and Elizabeth ('Lizzie') – baby Hetty being as yet unborn. One of the daughters noticed Mary's advertisement and said to her father, 'Come on, Daddy – let's go down (to Dorset) and see this place!' They were tenants for ten years, and it was in the idyllic setting of Dunshay that the Baynes children grew up.

Leslie Baynes's background was as follows: the son of a publisher, he was born on 23 March, 1902 at Church Road, Barnes, West London and educated at Gresham's School, Holt in Norfolk where he was a boarder. In 1916, two years into the Great War when he was aged only fourteen, he was already an aircraft enthusiast and took a keen interest in the exploits of the Royal Flying Corps which, with the Royal Naval Air Service, was to be the precursor of the Royal Air Force.

One day whilst the family was holidaying at St Margaret's Bay near Dover, the young Leslie announced to his mother that he did not wish to return to boarding school. 'Why not?', she enquired. 'Because there is a war on, and I want to do something useful'. 'Oh yes, and what is that?'. He then told his mother about the Aircraft Manufacturing Company 'Airco' – a large concern employing around 5000 people based at Hendon (now Greater London). She promised to look into it, and before he knew it she had signed him up to begin an apprenticeship there. The boy was delighted. He found lodgings at Hampstead Garden Suburb from where he cycled the 4 miles into work each morning; starting at 8 a.m. Now would commence an outstanding career in which he would bring his unique genius to bear on revolutionising the design and development of aircraft in a variety of different ways.

For the next two years Baynes worked as assistant to an experimental engineer at Airco. The office was a wooden hut (adjacent to which was a workshop with its own resident mechanic) where designs and modifications were made for the military aircraft which were being manufactured on site for the war effort. In order to appreciate fully Baynes's contribution as a pioneer of aeronautical engineering, it is necessary to be aware of progress hitherto made in this field.

Geoffrey de Havilland.
Photo: BAE SYSTEMS.

Airco's chief aircraft designer was Geoffrey de Havilland, twenty years older than Baynes, and like him born to a non-engineering family; his father being a curate. From an early age, however, he and his elder brother Ivon's consuming interest was making mechanical models.

In 1900 de Havilland enrolled for three years at the Crystal Palace Engineering School, and then spent two years as a student apprentice at the turbine engineering works of Willans and Robinson in Rugby, Staffordshire, before becoming in 1905, draughtsman in the drawing office of the Wolseley Tool and Motor-Car Company at Adderley Park, Birmingham. A turning point in his life came when he and his brother Ivon saw their first air balloon rising in the sky. Now the possibility that man might one day conquer the air seriously entered their minds.

Leaders in the field of aviation were the Wright brothers – Wilbur and Orville – from Ohio in the U.S.A, who on 7 December, 1903 (having designed and built a lightweight petrol engine for the purpose), made the first powered flight in history. Having learned of the subsequent exploits of Wilbur Wright, who in 1908 at Auvours, near Le Mans in France, made over one hundred flights, Geoffrey de Havilland was 'Seized with an ambition' to design and build his own aeroplane. This he did, with the sum of £1000 given to him by his grandfather. In fact, he designed not only the aircraft – a single-engined biplane – but also its engine! It took to the skies in December 1909, the same year that French aviator Louis Bleriot made the first powered flight across the English Channel.

De Havilland then built a second aircraft, which was purchased by a friend Fred Green, engineer in charge of design at H.M. Army Balloon Factory at Farnborough, Hampshire, who offered him a job there in aircraft design and development. The Balloon Factory was subsequently renamed the 'Army Aircraft Factory', and in 1912, the 'Royal Aircraft Factory' – reflecting the change in emphasis from balloons to aircraft.

Early in 1914, when de Havilland's job at Farnborough came to an end, George Holt Thomas, founder of Airco at Hendon, invited him to be designer and pilot to the company. In August of that year, the Great War broke out. At the end of that month, de Havilland, a member of the Royal Flying Corps Reserve was recalled from flying patrols off the east coast of Scotland to Airco. The various aircraft designed by him there would have a significant influence on the outcome of the Great War; and Leslie Baynes, now learning the techniques of draughtsmanship and aircraft design could not have had a more inspiring role model than he.

൭൭

When the war ended in November 1918, Airco hoped to convert to the production of civil aircraft. Alas, the orders failed to materialise, and in 1919, it was taken over by the Birmingham Small Arms Company, and aircraft manufacturing ceased altogether.

De Havilland and some friends of his from Airco responded by creating in 1920 (at the Stag Lane Aerodrome, Edgware), the de Havilland Aircraft Company which went on to produce machines culminating in the 'Comet' – the world's first commercial jet airliner – which went into service in 1958 on the transatlantic route.

൭൭

Leslie Baynes became expert in adapting existing designs to improve their efficiency and in 1919 he patented the first automatic variable-pitch propeller or 'airscrew' – the pitch being the angle at which the blades of a propeller meet the air. This gave the pilot a choice when deciding the relative merits of upward lift and forward thrust.

Between 1924 and 1927 Baynes worked for Short Brothers, a company founded by Eustace and Oswald Short, who were subsequently joined by the third brother Horace. They had begun in 1898 by manufacturing balloons, then Wright biplanes (under licence) – thus becoming the world's first commercial manufacturers of aircraft; and in 1911, float-planes (where the wheels of the aircraft are replaced by floats). Between the wars Short Brothers turned their attention to building the first airliner flying boats (purpose-built always to land on water). These were the days before airfields were in universal existence, and it was far more common for an aircraft to land on a river or a lake, than on land: hence their importance.

As an employee of Short Brothers, Baynes was made responsible for the aerodynamics of the Short 'Calcutta', a flying boat of all-metal construction, powered by three 525h.p. Bristol Jupiter engines, designed to fly long-distance. Imperial Airways (founded March 1924) ordered five of these machines to cover the Mediterranean section of the England-India air route, and the Nile section of the England-Africa route. One of Baynes's consuming interests however, was in the field of glider design.

In 1931, Leslie Baynes went into partnership with a Mr E.D. Abbott (who owned a coach building company) in order to build gliders – 'sailplanes' to Baynes's design. They met with immediate success when in the same year at Tottenhoe in Bedfordshire, 'Scud I', piloted by Flight Lieutenant E. Mole, became the first British glider to soar for one hour. Now, everybody wanted a 'Scud', and when Baynes attended an international gliding show in Yorkshire in 1932 he was delighted to see that all the sailplanes gliding over the moors were Scud IIs – also designed by him. In 1933, a 'Scud II', piloted this time by Mungo Buxton, broke the British altitude record for gliders when it reached a height of 8750 feet.

'Scud II', the sailplane designed by L.E. Baynes and manufactured at the Abbott-Baynes sailplane works at Farnham, Surrey.

Photo: L.E. Baynes.

In 1934 Baynes was approached by his friend Sir John Carden who at that time was technical director of Vickers-Armstrong Ltd. Sir John was himself a flier and had adapted the engine of a Ford motor car to power light aircraft.

Although Sir John had an aeroplane of his own his intention was to own a sailplane; but he did not like the idea of having to depend on a launching catapult whenever he wished to go 'soaring'. He therefore asked Baynes to produce a sailplane powered by an auxiliary engine, with power sufficient to lift it off the ground and to an altitude sufficient for the purpose. Baynes accepted the challenge and calculated that such a sailplane would require significantly larger wingspans than the Scuds. However, a two-stroke 'Villiers' engine of a mere 250 cc, generating 9 hp, driving a 'pusher' propeller would supply all the power that was necessary. In order to accommodate the engine and propeller, Baynes designed the fuselage with a neck linking it to the cantilever wing above. Also the engine had to be mounted in the inverted position to keep the propeller clear of the fuselage, and the cylinder head had to be hinged to the fuselage neck in order for the engine to be retracted in flight to reduce drag.

The 'Carden-Baynes Auxiliary': 1935, a sailplane with a retractable 2-stroke engine, designed by Baynes.

Photo: L.E. Baynes.

The 'Carden-Baynes Auxiliary' as it was called, was constructed entirely of wood – the fuselage being built of planked plywood and spruce, with more plywood covering the leading edges of the wings and fabric covering the trailing edges. The woodwork was coated in natural varnish with clear dope on the wings and tail surfaces. The wings were detachable so that in a few minutes the aircraft could be dismantled and loaded onto a trailer. To check the stability and controls the first flight was made in the traditional way by catapulting the Auxiliary into the air without using the engine. It was a great success; and on 5 May, 1935, the sailplane was exhibited at the Royal Aeronautical Society meeting at Fairey Aviation Company's Heathrow Aerodrome (London).

On 8 August, 1935, at Woodley Aerodrome at Reading, the time had come to test the Auxiliary with engine. Everything went according to plan. The machine, with pilot Dr J.P. Dewsbery at the controls, built up speed and left the ground, then circled slowly to 5000 feet when those on the ground heard the engine stop. The engine duly retracted into the fuselage and after several silent circuits of the airfield, the Auxiliary made a perfect landing. The event had taken fifteen minutes, the Villiers engine – which, with its fuel tank weighed a mere 50 lbs – had consumed less than a gallon of petrol, and the world's first motorised sailplane, designed by Leslie Baynes, had made its maiden flight.

There were two sad sequels: the first when Sir John Carden was killed later in the year as the aircraft in which he was travelling back from a business meeting in Belgium crashed on the North Downs at Tatsfield in Surrey. The second tragedy was when Augustus Charles Lennox, 7th Duke of Grafton, who had placed an order for a second Auxiliary for himself in the September of 1935, was killed in a racing car accident in Ireland. (Grafton had formerly served as Hon. Equerry to Queen Victoria, King Edward VII, and King George V). In 1982, forty-seven years after it was built, the original Auxiliary, now based at Dunstable, was still airworthy!

In 1937, Baynes designed and built the 'Baynes Bee' – the first twin-engined pusher monoplane with 'wing-buried' engines. A tiny two-seater aircraft a mere 29ft. 10ins. long, built by Carden Baynes Aircraft Ltd at Heston (Greater London), it was powered by two 40 horse-power Carden engines and underwent its maiden flight in April 1937. Sadly, the forthcoming Second World War would put an end to its further development.

13

Further Inventions and Innovations: Variable Geometry (or 'Swing Wing'): Dunshay Years

In 1938, when Baynes was aviation advisor to the Alan Muntz Company at Heston, he became involved in a project to adapt a multi-screw (i.e. multi-propeller) gas turbine system for use as the propulsion unit for a large, long range flying boat with sufficient capacity to carry 100 passengers. The pressurised hull would enable the aircraft to fly at high altitude.

In those days however, pressurisation of the aircraft's hull was not the norm; so the gas turbine (where a rotary motor is driven by the vanes of the wheel turned by expanding hot air) had the advantage over the jet engine (the basic design of which was patented by a young R.A.F officer called Frank Whittle in 1930) in both performance and fuel economy, since it is when flying at high altitude and high speed that jets are most efficient. In this case, the Baynes-Muntz flying boat would be driven by 6 wing-mounted turbine units driving propellers supplied with combustion gases obtained from generators located in the hull.

In that year Baynes designed and patented the first Vertical Take Off and Landing (V/TOL) swivel turbine 'Heliplane'. This concept was first described by French artillery officer Rene Lorin who, in 1907, set out in an article published in the magazine *L'Aerophile* on 1 September, his vision of an aeroplane powered by two engines set in line; one on either side of the fuselage. The exhaust nozzles would be hinge-mounted, and could therefore be directed downwards to achieve a near-vertical take off before being slowly swivelled into the horizontal position for flight.

The first V/TOL aircraft was the British Hawker Siddely 'Harrier' ground-attack fighter which was test-flown in 1966, Powered by ducted fan let engines with swivelling nozzles, it came into service with the R.A.F in 1969, and subsequently with the United States Marines, the Harrier saw service in the Falklands War of 1982 and in the Gulf War of 1991.

During the Second World War Baynes built, for the Ministry of Supply an experimental aircraft without a tail – the so-called 'Flying Wing'. (The idea had originally come from the German engineer Hugo Junkers, who took out a patent for it in February 1910). In the Flying Wing, all the necessary components would be housed including crew, passengers, engines, fuel. As for its payload, it was envisaged that such an aircraft would be ideally suited to transport army tanks to the battlefield. The design eventually came to fruition in the shape of the British Avro-Vulcan (the world's first 4-engined delta-winged jet bomber which made its maiden flight on 30 August, 1952) and in the American F-117A 'Stealth' fighter-bomber used in the Gulf War of 1991. Baynes was also instrumental in the conversion of American built 'Boston' bombers into 'Havoc' night fighter aircraft which carried the Turbinlight airborne searchlight – reputed to be five times brighter than the sun!

'Boston' bomber with searchlight for night fighting. L.E. Baynes (2nd from right) and Chief Engineer Benson (right). Photo: N.W.E. Baynes.

Other inventions of his included a glide-bomb, submarine, high-lift research aircraft, aircraft seats, speed range indicator, domestic furniture, bicycle wheels, and even childrens' toys! However, Baynes's most breath-taking design concept in the field of aviation was yet to come.

෴

1890 marked the year of the first flight of French engineer Clement Ader's bat-wing steam-powered aeroplane, the 'Eole'. In the year Ader patented an aircraft one of whose features was a limited degree of in-flight 'variable sweep'. The perceived advantage of such an aircraft was that it would be capable of flying at a wide range of speed – fast with the wings swept back (when there would be less drag), and slower with the wings outstretched.

One of the problems of flying 'variable geometry' ('swing wing') aircraft, however, is that depending on its speed, the aerodynamic centre of gravity alters relative to the actual centre of gravity, which makes it necessary to alter the trim (balance) to avoid the machine either rearing up or plunging into the ground.

When, after the Second World War, the Bell Company of the United States built a variable sweep aircraft, they allowed for this by using an on-board system of water pumps and reservoirs. However, the aircraft was not a success, and crashed.

෴

Barnes Wallis, born in 1887, was the designer of airships, the Wellesley and the Wellington bombers, and the 'bouncing bombs' which destroyed the German Mohne and Eder dams on the River Ruhr in 1943. The son of a surgeon, he had begun his working life as a marine engineer with J.S. White and Co,

Barnes Wallis. Photo: BAE SYSTEMS

Ltd at Cowes, on the Isle of Wight. In 1913 Wallis joined the Aviation Section of Vickers, the engineering company located at Erith in Kent, (later to become Vickers Armstrong Ltd). He soon became Chief Assistant in the Airship Department, and in 1924, Chief Designer of the Airship R-100. The crash of Airship R-101 in France however, signalled the end of airship production in Britain.

Wallis now produced the 'Swallow', a tail-less Flying Wing but more advanced than that produced by Baynes in that its wings, in the shape of a delta, were hinged so that at speed they could be swept back, to make it more aerodynamic. In 1955, an 8 foot long rocket-propelled version of the Swallow flew successfully at 2.5 times the speed of sound (almost 2000 mph) from the artillery range at Larkhill on Salisbury Plain. However, the Ministry of Supply showed the same indifference to Wallis as they had to Baynes, when he had attempted to interest them in the Flying Wing.

∾

Now it was Baynes's turn to make a contribution to this exciting new world of variable geometry. He calculated the range of speed which would be required for a fighter aircraft to be able to fly at supersonic speeds and at the same time land on a relatively short runway, such as the deck of an aircraft carrier. His designs for such an aircraft included a tailplane, whose wings and fin could vary their sweep in conjunction with the mainplane. In this way the trim could be adjusted to cope with changes in the aerodynamic centre of gravity, without the necessity of having to move ballast around the aircraft.

However, when in 1949, Baynes sent his plans to the Ministry of Supply, they immediately classified them as 'Top Secret' and forbade him from reading a paper on the project to the Royal Aeronautical Society. After this, despite strenuous efforts by Baynes to interest his employers Vickers, and the Ministry in the project, he like Wallis, had the mortification of seeing his plans abandoned. Nevertheless, following extensive mathematical calculations and exhaustive wind-tunnel trials, Baynes, on 12 February, 1952, filed the patent for this 'High Speed Aircraft having Wings with Variable Sweepback'.

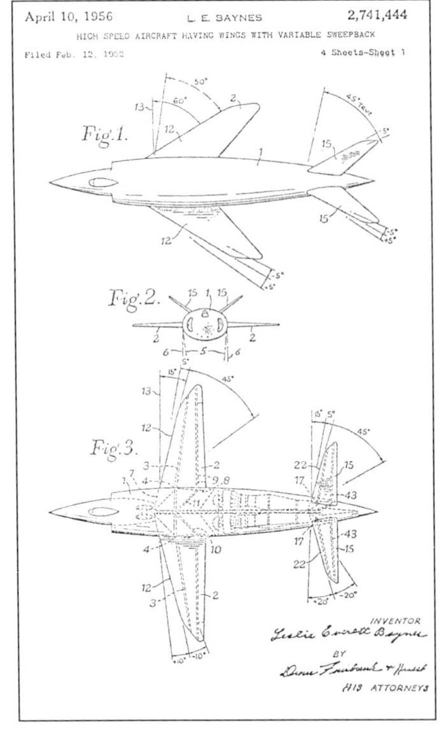

L.E. Baynes's patent for 'High Speed Aircraft having Wings with Variable Sweepback' – filed 12 February, 1952.
Photo: N.W.E. Baynes.

It was left to the Americans to exploit the concept of 'Swing Wing', which they did with the successful launch of the General Dynamics F-111A – the world's first operational variable geometry combat aircraft. It made its debut flight from Fort Worth, Texas on 21 December, 1964 with its wings fixed at a sweepback angle of 26 degrees. The following month it made its first flight with the wings at varying angles of sweepback ranging from 16 to 72.5 degrees. The aircraft went into service with the U.S. Air Force and saw service in the Vietnam War.

Author, Major Oliver Stewart posed the question, why is variable sweep so important when the supersonic Concorde could do without it? He concludes that the aircraft performs well at low speeds, when 'cocked up' in the pre-landing position, and up to Mach 2 (1350 mph) which is its cruising speed. However, for it to achieve speeds above Mach 2,2, then he believes that variable sweep would become a necessity.

Baynes now formed a new company, Baynes Engineering Ltd., at Hurn Airport near Bournemouth where he designed and manufactured airliner equipment for leading aircraft companies. This was within motoring distance of Dunshay Manor. He and his family spent their summers at Buckshore beach in Swanage, swimming in the bracing waters of Swanage Bay and participating in the activities of the local sailing club.

L.E. Baynes on Studland beach in 1960.

Photo: N.W.E. Baynes.

In 1963–4 Baynes designed and patented a new form of hydrofoil boat: it being essentially a combination of hydrofoil (whereby the boat is raised from the water as its speed increases) and a hydroplane (whereby the vessel skims over the surface of the water). Having created a small hydrofoil for research purposes, he designed a larger one and submitted it to the Ministry. However, as with his variable sweep aircraft, all the Ministry did was, in his own words, to 'pay me the dubious honour of classifying it "Top Secret"'. It would therefore be some years before this idea was developed.

The Baynes hydrofoil high speed experimental craft, being tested in Swanage Bay, airline pilot Michael Martin at the helm.

Photo: N.W.E. Baynes.

In an address to the Swanage Round Table, Baynes told the assembled company that to be living at that time meant that they were the luckiest people in the history of the world. More than any other form of animal life, man with his ingenuity, resourcefulness and invention had made the world his own. It was their (the Round Tablers') good fortune, in the lottery of life, to have been born just at the time when man had made his supreme conquest – space, he said. Man had just conquered the moon, and the prospect of reaching out to the stars was now a technical possibility.

In the latter part of his life, when he was living in a rest home in Swanage, Baynes was greatly amused to hear himself affectionately referred to by his nickname 'Baron', when he ventured out to the shops or took his daily 'constitutional' walk along the Swanage sea front.

Of an evening he was invariably to be found in the lounge of the Grand Hotel, attired in jumper, corduroys, and polished, brown leather shoes, supping his favourite drink of Guinness and reliving his adventures with an always eager audience of local people, to whom he was something of a legend. This was the case, even for those who had never flown in an aeroplane!

Leslie Baynes, that remarkable inventor and innovator, died on March 18, 1989, at the age of eighty-six. He is buried in Godlingstone Cemetery, Swanage.

14

Dunshay Lives on...

In her time, Mary Spencer Watson has carved in wood, modelled in clay and even attempted to sculpt in Purbeck marble, which because of its hardness she found extremely difficult to work. She therefore confesses that stone is her favourite medium, in particular, Purbeck Stone.

The geology of the Isle of Purbeck is diverse, and this is reflected in the many varieties of Purbeck stone which are to be found here. To the north are soft sands and clays, then hard chalk, then sand and soft clay and finally, in the southern coastal area, hard limestones.

The Reverend Hutchins gives a detailed description of the different varieties of stone which are encountered at various levels beneath the surface, with illuminating comments as to their nature and usefulness. They occur in veins laid down prehistorically as sedimentary maritime deposits, and are separated by earth.

The WHITE RAG is of poor quality and fit only for foundations. Then comes the TOAD'S EYE, so called because the convex fossils found in it resemble toads' eyes. Beneath this is another layer of RAG and then comes the ROACH, which was formerly used for tombstones.

Newly-weds aboard stone waggon.
Photo: David Haysom.

Deeper down is LEPER, its name deriving from its colour, which resembles the skin of a leprous person, Then comes SOFTBED, HARDBED, MOCK HARD BED and BACKING BED – the latter being useful only to fill in the cavities of double-skinned walls. The RIAL is used for kerbs and is hard and durable. Then comes the TOP GALLANT RAG which is so hard as to merit the name 'DEVIL'S BED'. The FREE STONE RAG and the UNDER RAG are of good quality. The LEAD BED and SHINGLE beneath are of little use, but the GRUB is good.Deeper still is to be found better quality stone, such as the FREESTONE ROACH, GREY BED, and THORNBACK. LIAS, AND LIAS RAG are not of the best; then comes the DOWN VEIN (good) and CINDER – 'No tool can work this. Gunpowder alone can affect it'. Deeper still is the BUTTONS layer (no use), then FEATHER, CAP, FIVE BEDS (so-called because it splits readily into five pieces) and WHITE BED, which are all good. The TOMBSTONE beneath is useless as it often contains flints, as is the RAW PUDDING, KNIFE AND SHEARS.

~

For sculpture, Mary prefers PURBECK FREESTONE, PURBECK PORTLAND stone and PURBECK BURR. However, she often imports stone from elsewhere, using for example: PORTLAND stone, CLIPSHAM stone from Rutland and HAM HILL stone from Martock in Somerset.

A happy event occurred on the 11 February, 1997 – Shrove Tuesday – when, to Mary's great joy, she was made an Honorary Freeman of the 'Ancient Order of Purbeck Marblers and Stonecutters'.

~

Mary has two ways of working. She may already have an idea, which she translates first into a small sketch and then, after some thought, into a clay model. If on the other hand she needs to be inspired, she will take her trailer up to the quarry and 'shop around' for an interesting block of stone. Then, back at her workshop, she hoists it up aloft on her gantry-crane so that, with the flick of a finger, she can turn it round and round or up on end. Having lived with it for anything between a few hours or several days, an idea for a 'creation' takes root in her mind. She thinks of it as a two way process, often finding that it is the stone which suggests something to her, rather than the other–way round!

'Lady of the Rocks' by Mary Spencer-Watson – Prince Albert Gardens, Swanage – 1992.

Photo: Mary Spencer Watson.

Swanage Town Council has created on the sloping hillside of the Prince Albert Gardens, a classical theatre in an atmospheric setting where, across Swanage Bay, can be seen the mighty cliffs of Ballard Down which terminate at Handfast Point, When the Wareham District Council asked Mary to create a sculpture for the site she conceived the idea of a female figure looking out to sea. The figure would have a swan at her feet (swans being considered appropriate for Swanage!) and a sea-bird on her shoulder. She would be made of Purbeck stone; and all around her were rocky shores and cliffs – hence her title, 'The Lady of the Rocks'!

The background to the composition of this piece goes back to Mary's childhood at Studland, when she used to ride her donkey to Handfast Point, where there are pinnacles of rock nicknamed 'Old Harry' and 'Old Harry's Wife', protruding from the sea. Whilst her father George painted, she would venture into the wood which in spring-time was full of bluebells; or stand near the edge of the cliffs and gaze down in wonder at the gulls which soared below. That place made an enormous impression on her.

'Figure of a Mason' by Mary Spencer Watson – Church of St George, Langton Matravers.

Photo: Mary Spencer Watson.

The inspiration for 'Figure of a Mason', which stands outside the parish church of St George at Langton Matravers, again goes back to Mary's childhood, when in 1923 she became captivated by stone. This time it was Langton Parish Council who invited her to create a 'Millennium Figure', in commemoration of the stone industry. The result was a sculpture with which she has tremendous empathy.

ᘓ

'Jesus and Mary' by Mary Spencer-Watson – the Morning Chapel, Salisbury Cathedral.

Photo: The Dean.

Ecclesiastical sculpture Is perhaps the subject closest to Mary's heart, and amongst her most intriguing works are 'The Four Beasts of Ezechiel' which stand in the grounds of Wells Cathedral.

'I do not think of God as being an old man with a beard!' she says, 'but I believe there is a "Principle" present in the universe which we can become aware of.'

ᘓ

So Dunshay Manor lives on.... Will the next millennium see Dunshay providing a residence for people of such interest, influence, and creativity as it has done over the past thousand years? Surely one day there will be further chapters to add to the colourful history of Dunshay Manor and its extraordinary inhabitants!

Bibliography

Caffery, Edward. *A Church and a Chapitle*. Edward Caffery, 1992.

Field, J. *Place Names of Great Britain and Ireland*. David & Charles, 1980.

Hutchins, Reverend John, M.A. *The History and Antiquities of the County of Dorset*. 1774.

Jowitt, R.L.P. *Salisbury*. B.T. Batsford Ltd., 1951.

Keelan, J. *Shrewsbury Abbey* – Earl Roger de Montgomerie.

Shrewsbury Abbey Restoration Project, 1990.

Mills, A.D. *Dorset Place Names*. Roy Gasson Associates, 1986.

National Trust. *Corfe Castle – 1000 years of History*. 1986.

Owen, H. and Blakeway, J.C. *A History of Shrewsbury*. 1825, Volume 1. Shrewsbury Museum Service.

Ross, Reverend Ian. *Shrewsbury Abbey – A Benedictine Foundation*.

Smith, Lucy Toulmin. *The Itinerary of John Leland*. George Bell and Sons, London, 1907.

Wordsworth, Chr., M.A. *Ceremonies and Processions of the Cathedral Church of Salisbury*. Cambridge University Press, 1901.

Crookshank, Edgar M., M.B. *History and Pathology of Vaccination*. H.K. Lewis, London, 1889.

Curwen, E. Cecil. *The Journal of Gideon Mantel*. Oxford University Press, 1940.

Hayward, Nina. *Yetminster and Beyond*. Yetminster Local History Society.

Hunt, John A. *Benjamin Jesty – a True Pioneer*. The Pharmaceutical Journal, 19 and 26 December, 1998.

'The *Lancet*', 14.9.1862.

Lewer, David, and Smale, Dennis. *Swanage Past*. Phillimore & Co Ltd., 1994.

United States Government Printing Office, Washington. *The Ship's Medicine Chest and First Aid at Sea*. 1947.

Wallace, E. Marjorie, M.A. *The First Vaccinator*. Anglebury-Bartlett Ltd., 1981.

Windridge, Nina. *The Prebends of Yetminster*. Yetminster Local History Society, 1999.

Bayley, Mrs *The Life and Letters of Anna Sewell.* James Nisbet & Co., London, 1889.
Wortley, Laura. *Lucy Kemp-Welch 1869–1958. The Spirit of the Horse.* Antique Collectors Club, 1996.

ᘓ

Baynes, Leslie E., A.F.R.Ae.S. 'The Carden-Baynes Auxiliary'. *Aeroplane Monthly.* November 1982.
Briggs, Asa. *Dictionary of Twentieth Century World Biography.* Oxford University Press, 1992.
Bullock, Alan. *Great Lives of the Twentieth Century.* Peerage Books, 1988.
De Havilland, Sir Geoffrey. *Sky Fever.* Airlife Publishing Ltd., 1979.
Gibbs-Smith, Charles H. *Aviation – an Historical Survey: Science Museum.* Her Majesty's Stationery Office, London, 1985.
Morse, William, MRAeS. *Geoffrey de Havilland,* 1882–1965. Published by 'Wing Span'.
Murpigo, J.E. *Barnes Wallis.* Longmans, 1972.
Poole and Dorset Advertiser. Aviation Genius who lived so modestly. Article by 'Tilly Whim', March 30 1989.
Smith, G. Geoffrey, M.B.E. *Gas Turbines and Jet Propulsion.* Iliffe and Sons Ltd., London, 1955.
Stewart, Oliver. *British Pioneer of Variable Geometry. Times* Supplement on British Aviation, 10 June 1965.
Taylor, John. *The Lore of Flight.* Nelson, 1973.
Taylor, Michael and Mondey, David. *The Guinness Book of Aircraft.* Guinness Publishing Ltd., 1992.
Taylor, Michael J.H. *Jane's Encyclopaedia of Aviation.* Bracken Books, London, 1980.
The Times. L.E. Baynes. Obituary, 18 March, 1989. Source News International Database.

ᘓ

Brocklebank, Joan. *The Dollings of Dunshay.* Essay, 1983.
Compton, Michael. *George Spencer Watson.* Southampton Art Gallery, Department of Leisure Services, 1981.
Compton, Susan. *Mary Spencer Watson.* An Ellipsis production, 1991.
Davies, Peter. *Art in Poole and Dorset.* Poole Historical Trust. The Phaidon Press Ltd., 1987.